What Every Teacher Should Know About

Diverse Learners

What Every Teacher Should Know About...

What Every Teacher Should Know About
Diverse Learners

What Every Teacher Should Know About
Student Motivation

What Every Teacher Should Know About
Learning, Memory, and the Brain

What Every Teacher Should Know About
Instructional Planning

What Every Teacher Should Know About
Effective Teaching Strategies

What Every Teacher Should Know About
Classroom Management and Discipline

What Every Teacher Should Know About
Student Assessment

What Every Teacher Should Know About
Special Learners

What Every Teacher Should Know About
Media and Technology

What Every Teacher Should Know About
The Profession and Politics of Teaching

DONNA WALKER TILESTON

What Every Teacher Should Know About
Diverse Learners

CORWIN PRESS
A Sage Publications Company
Thousand Oaks, California

For information:

Corwin Press
A Sage Publications Company
2455 Teller Road
Thousand Oaks, California 91320
www.corwinpress.com

Sage Publications Ltd.
6 Bonhill Street
London EC2A 4PU
United Kingdom

Sage Publications India Pvt. Ltd.
B-42, Panchsheel Enclave
Post Box 4109
New Delhi 110 017 India

Printed in the United States of America

Library of Congress Cataloging-in-Publication Data
Tileston, Donna Walker.
What every teacher should know about diverse learners/
Donna Walker Tileston.
    p. cm.
(What every teacher should know about—; 1)
Includes bibliographical references and index.
ISBN 0-7619-3117-1 (paper)
    1. Multicultural education—United States—History.
2. Minorities—Education—United States—History. I. Title. II. Series.
LC1099.3.T55 2004
370.117—dc21   2003010242

This book is printed on acid-free paper.

03   04   05   06   07   10   9   8   7   6   5   4   3   2   1

Acquisitions Editor:	Faye Zucker
Editorial Assistant:	Stacy Wagner
Production Editor:	Diane S. Foster
Copy Editor:	Stacey Shimizu
Typesetter:	C&M Digitals (P) Ltd.
Proofreader:	Mary Meagher
Indexer:	Will Ragsdale
Cover Designer:	Tracy E. Miller
Production Artist:	Lisa Miller

Contents

About the Author

Donna Walker Tileston, Ed.D., is a veteran teacher of 27 years and the president of Strategic Teaching and Learning, a consulting firm that provides services to schools throughout the United States and Canada. Also an author, Donna's publications include *Strategies for Teaching Differently: On the Block or Not* (Corwin Press, 1998), *Innovative Strategies of the Block Schedule* (Bureau of Education and Research [BER], 1999), and *Ten Best Teaching Practices: How Brain Research, Learning Styles, and Standards Define Teaching Competencies* (Corwin Press, 2000), which has been on Corwin's best-seller list since its first year in print.

Donna received her B.A. from the University of North Texas, her M.A. from East Texas State University, and her Ed.D. from Texas A & M University-Commerce. She may be reached at www.strategicteaching&learning.com or by e-mail at dwtileston@yahoo.com.

Acknowledgments

My sincere thanks go to my Acquisitions Editor, Faye Zucker, for her faith in education and what this information can do to help all children be successful. Without Faye, these books would not have been possible.

I had the best team of editors around: Diane Foster, Stacy Wagner, and Stacey Shimizu. You took my words and you gave them power. Thank you.

Thanks to my wonderful Board Chairman at Strategic Teaching and Learning, Dulany Howland: Thank you for sticking with me in the good times and the tough spots. Your expertise and friendship have been invaluable.

*To my aunt, Betty Walker Smith, who has dedicated
her teaching career to working with the Native American
children of the Southwest.*

Introduction

The Supreme Court's 1954 decision in Brown v. Board of Education of Topeka, Kansas, *made equal access to public education the law of the land. With each decade we have increased the proportion of the U.S. population in school, including children from more diverse socio-culture and economic backgrounds, and diversified the kinds of educational programs offered. But these accomplishments have fallen far short of the vision of a universal school system that provides all children with equal access to success in school.*

—M. C. Wang and J. A. Kovach, *Bridging the Achievement Gap in Urban Schools*

As the economy, resources, and affluence of the city have moved to the suburbs, we have been left with many large cities whose inner-city area is a myriad of crumbling buildings, graffiti, and the poor who cannot afford to leave. Add to that a struggling economy and the lack of resources available, and we have an educational system that, despite its best efforts, cannot provide equal access to success. Teachers are leaving the field in droves either to enter a different field or to follow the resources to the suburbs of the city. Why not? Our society measures the success of schools and its personnel on test scores—often single test scores. Even when the measurement includes other factors, such as dropout rates, attendance rates, and the percentage of students taking advanced courses, the complex problems of teaching a diverse population of urban students from ethnic and language minority backgrounds remains a factor usually not considered.

Throughout this book, we will examine how we got to this place and look at some of the best research available for helping to narrow and eventually close the achievement gap for minority students. While many of the solutions for urban schools are a matter of combining resources from state and local communities, including health and dental care, family assistance, and the collaboration of community leaders in the decision making process, this book focuses on what the classroom teacher can do to help ensure that these students learn— and learn at a high level.

Brain research has afforded us insights into new ways to reach these students. We now know, for instance, that inner-city students learn better when visual and kinesthetic approaches are used than they do when a traditional curriculum based on verbal teaching is employed (Payne, 2001). English language learners may not have the language acquisition skills necessary for processing a great deal of data in a verbal format. By incorporating visual tools into the curriculum and by providing a variety of teaching strategies, we can reach these students at a level never before possible.

The Vocabulary Summary of this book contains terms often used in conjunction with working with urban learners. Form 0.1 provides a list of the vocabulary words for this book. In the space provided, write your definition of the word at this time. After you have read this book, go back to your original answers to see if you have changed your mind about your definitions.

In addition, I am providing a pre-test to help you identify your own knowledge of the vocabulary that will be used in this volume. At the end of the book are a post-test and the answers to the test for your self-assessment.

Form 0.1   Vocabulary List for Diverse Learners

Vocabulary	Your Definition	Your Revised Definition
At-risk students		
Bias		
Classroom climate		
Direct instruction		
Diversity		
English language learners		
Ethnicity		
Ethnocentrism		
Exceptionality		
Heterogeneous grouping		
Hidden rules of society		
Imaginary audience		
Intrinsic motivation		
Learned helplessness		
Learning environment		

(Continued)

Form 0.1   Continued

Locus of control		
Melting-pot theory		
Minority group		
Modality		
Motivation		
Multicultural education		
Nondiscriminatory testing		
Personal fable		
Self-concept		
Self-efficacy		
Self-esteem		
Self-fulfilling prophecy		
Socioeconomic status		
Self-talk		
Voices		

Vocabulary Pre-Test

Instructions: For each question given, choose the best answer or answers. More than one answer may be correct.

1. The belief that one group of people is superior to other groups is called . . .
   A. The melting-pot theory
   B. Ethnocentrism
   C. Exceptionality
   D. Diversity

2. Diane Madden is a teacher at East Middle School, where she teaches eighth-grade American History. Ms. Madden talked with teachers from the seventh grade prior to the beginning of school and asked them to give her their opinion about which students will be A students and which students will not put forth effort in her classroom this year. Ms. Madden's actions are most probably connected to . . .
   A. Ethnocentrism
   B. The melting-pot theory
   C. Exceptionality
   D. Self-fulfilling prophecies

3. Students who come from generational poverty are usually . . .
   A. Auditory learners
   B. Visual learners
   C. Kinesthetic learners
   D. Declarative learners

4. Students who believe that they just have bad luck in school may be suffering from poor . . .
   A. Diversity
   B. Locus of control
   C. Self-efficacy
   D. Self-esteem

5. Students who believe that they can succeed because they have succeeded in the past are practicing . . .
   A. The auditory modality
   B. Locus of control
   C. Self-efficacy
   D. Extrinsic motivation

6. Teachers who tell students that they will get candy for good work are using . . .
   A. Locus of control
   B. Intrinsic motivation
   C. Self-fulfilling prophecy
   D. Extrinsic motivation

7. Marci, a student in South High School, has experimented with drugs with her friends. Although she has been told that the drugs are addicting and can lead to harmful behavior, Marci believes that she is immune to bad things happening to her. Marci is practicing . . .
   A. Imaginary audience
   B. Locus of control
   C. Personal fable
   D. Self-fulfilling prophecy

8. Students who have lived in situations of great stress over time often experience . . .
   A. Imaginary audience
   B. Self-fulfilling prophecy
   C. Exceptionality
   D. Learned helplessness

9. Teachers who teach in a variety of formats so that they teach to all races and ethnicities are practicing . . .
   A. Contextualization
   B. Ethnocentrism
   C. Pluralism
   D. Indirect teaching

10. English language learners (ELLs) . . .
    A. Are considered to have low socioeconomic status
    B. Speak a language other than English as their primary language
    C. Are often shy in class
    D. Have low intrinsic motivation to learn

11. Raul is in Mr. Vasquez's math class at Moors Middle School. Raul is struggling because he cannot grasp some of the math concepts being taught. Mr. Vasquez has added graphic organizers to help students like Raul learn more successfully. Raul is probably what kind of learner?
    A. Kinesthetic
    B. Visual
    C. Auditory
    D. Dual skill

12. Which of the following are used to determine at-risk students?
    A. Low socioeconomic status
    B. ELL status
    C. Previous failure
    D. Ethnicity

13. Marty came to school on Friday with red streaks in his hair (just like his two best friends). Marty is exhibiting . . .
    A. Personal fable
    B. Self-efficacy
    C. Imaginary audience
    D. Self-fulfilling prophecy

14. When students become what we expect them to become, it is called . . .
    A. An imaginary audience
    B. A self-fulfilling prophecy
    C. Self-efficacy
    D. Personal fable

15. Most students in the classroom are which type of learners?
    A. Auditory
    B. Visual
    C. Kinesthetic
    D. Intrinsic

16. *Diversity* means . . .
    A. Differences
    B. Ethnicity
    C. Exceptionality
    D. Bias

17. The belief that people moving to this country should become like us is called . . .
    A. Exceptionality
    B. Ethnocentrism
    C. Multicultural
    D. The melting-pot theory

18. Intrinsic motivation is triggered by . . .
    A. Relevance
    B. Stickers
    C. Emotions
    D. Relationships

19. Kelvin Waters has difficulty completing tasks once he begins. Research on which topic would be most helpful for him?
    A. The metacognitive system
    B. The self-system
    C. The cognitive system
    D. The procedural system

20. Which of the following is part of classroom climate?
    A. The lighting in the room
    B. The amount of tension in the room
    C. The way the room smells
    D. The socioeconomic status of the students

1

Influences

A teacher affects eternity. . . . She never knows where her influence stops

—Anonymous

There is an old story about the new teacher who is so excited about the first day of school. As she gets her room ready for the first day, she envisions a classroom of students eager to learn. Then, when the day finally arrives, she complains that someone sent her the wrong kids, because the students she was sent are not all eager to learn, not all ready to learn, and not all prepared to learn.

As a former administrator of mine used to say, "Parents are sending us the best they have." We do not have much control over the environment from which our students come, nor do we have much control over some of the adversity they must overcome to be successful. What we do have control over is seven to eight hours of their lives five days a week. During that time, we can give them the hope, the dreams, and the tools to make their lives meaningful. We really do affect eternity!

Diversity refers to differences. Today's learners are different in many ways, such as race, ethnicity, socioeconomic status, gender, learning modalities, cognitive development, social development, and the rate in which they take in information and retrieve it.

Each student in the classroom is unique in some way. A successful teacher recognizes that diversity may affect learning, and thus works toward a classroom in which diversity is celebrated and revered. In such a classroom, there is a conscious effort to help students recognize and respect differences; there is a sense of community. In this book, we will look at how we acquired these students and what we, as teachers, can do to make sure that there is an equal opportunity for success in the classroom.

BACK TO THE FUTURE

To understand students today, it is important to look at the recent past and some of the major influences in the world that have affected schools. This exercise will provide insight into why some of the things we try today do not work and why we cannot teach multimedia kids with the same techniques that we have used with homogeneous classrooms.

The 1950s

If you had been a teacher in the 1950s, most of your students would have come from families with traditional values. "Mothers stayed home and managed the home and children. Values of the home were reinforced through the church, school, and organizations" (Stratton, 1995). Your school building would probably look something like the factories of that time, and the factory model would certainly influence the way schools were run. Jensen (1998) says that the notion was "that we could bring everyone together in a single place and offer a standardized, 'conveyor belt' curriculum." That works if students are all alike, learn alike, and have no special needs.

Have you ever seen the old *I Love Lucy* episode in which Lucy and Ethel take jobs in a candy factory? That scenario is a pretty good analogy to the factory model of learning and why it just does not work. Just as Lucy and Ethel could not keep up with the pace as the conveyer belt changed speeds, so many students who have different needs and time restraints on learning cannot keep up either. The overall drop-out rate in the 1950s was around 30%. The labor market gladly took the drop-outs, because at that time the number of jobs for unskilled labor was about 30%.

The 1950s was also a time of major curriculum reform influenced by major events. Some of those events shook up the thinking and changed education forever. Stratton (1995) listed the major effects of the past on students today. Using their list, let's look at some of the influences from the 1950s.

Television. Television came into the homes of Americans in the 1950s, and with it came an introduction into a world much larger than the local neighborhood that had controlled their thinking. Students' idols went from the more traditional to the new-era idols of Rock-and-Roll. Until the events of September 11, 2001, in which airplanes were flown into New York's Twin Towers and the Pentagon, our heroes tended to be media idols. The events of that September morning and the subsequent fallout have led to the more traditional, pre-1950s heroes, such as firefighters, police officers, and superheroes.

Brown v. Board of Education. The 1954 *Brown v. Board of Education* case changed the precedent of the courts and changed the way we view separate versus equal. Up until this landmark case that went to the Supreme Court, courts had viewed separate facilities for education, public toilets, water fountains—the general way of life—as equal, so long as they were provided to both races. The Supreme Court, however, ruled that separate is *not* equal and ended segregation as a law. I said "as a law," because after all these years we are seeing a recurrence of segregation today based on poverty in our cities.

It is interesting to note that, while we have moved a long way from the days of separate is equal, we have come full circle back to a way of life in the urban cities that resembles the segregation of the 1950s. Wang and Kovach (1996) write, "As urban sprawl has taken place, those who could afford the suburbs have moved out of the inner cities with its high crime rate, poor air quality and decaying brick." This has left the inner cities to those who cannot leave for economic or other reasons. Inner-city students are often sent to older buildings wired well before the time of high technology. These schools often provide resources inferior to those of the new, more modern schools going up every year in the suburbs and the smaller communities outside the city. Wang and Kovach (1996) call this "residential segregation." They go on to say, "The movement of resources, jobs, and people from central city to the suburbs has created a hostile environment for children, families, and institutions embedded in the cities, including schools."

A study by Bartelt (1994) looked at the relationship between microsocial forces and educational accomplishment in the macroecology of 53 major cities across the country. The study concluded, "Inner schools are increasingly the schools of remnant populations and communities trapped by the economic irrelevance of their links to diminished labor markets." Because those left in the inner city are primarily minority groups, we seem to be back to the issue of equity underpinning *Brown v. Board of Education;* not just equity of buildings and resources, but of educational opportunities and outcomes as well. Williams (1996) says that "urban students' achievement reflects historical, social, and economic events: the dynamics of the relocation of industry from cities to suburbs, the transition to a postindustrial service economy, the history of racial segregation, and a new wave of large scale immigration."

The Sputnik Space Exploration Program. When Russia launched the first space exploration ship, called Sputnik, the United States quickly responded with a renewed interest in science and math. The fear was that American youth were falling behind in these two important subjects and that Russia might beat the United States in putting a man on the moon. Curriculum underwent major scrutiny and reform during this decade—one of the many reforms to come as the public looked increasingly toward weaknesses in the system.

The McCarthy Hearings. Senator Joseph McCarthy and the hearings he instigated moved paranoia to the forefront with the fear that there might be communists living next door. The question was, "Does the enemy live among us?" That feeling would be repeated in this new century, as Americans again would feel vulnerable.

The 1960s

The 1960s was a time of chaos:

Moral relativism and contradiction were the zeitgeist of the 1960's. Despite the fact that less than 20% of the Americans actually demonstrated or rioted, this decade was much more chaotic than its predecessor. Family and community, work and team ethics, respect for authority, Beatle mania, Woodstock, mantras and astrology, faded and torn blue jeans, long hair, free love, nonviolence, and drugs. And, we watched it all—together—on television—as the media magnified the reality. (Stratton, 1995)

Some of the events that shaped the 1960s and affected schools as well as other aspects of daily life include the following.

The Vietnam War. The Vietnam War had a dramatic effect on America's youth. With the war came the protesters and those who fled to Canada to avoid the draft. The country, divided over the war, was for the first time in history losing a war.

Assassinations. Americans watched, through the media of television, their heroes John F. Kennedy and Martin Luther King, Jr., being gunned down. Television and other media forms, over time, have been accused of desensitizing our youth to crime and violence. Sweeny (quoted in Stratton, 1995) says, there "can no longer be any doubt that heavy exposure to televised violence is one of the causes of aggressive behavior, crime, and violence in society."

Besides the fact that television has become increasingly violent over the years, it has also been a deterrent to family time, exercise, and other pastimes such as reading.

The Sexual Revolution. The new sexual freedom added to the loss of innocence.

Behavioral Theory. According to Jensen (1998), the dominant theory of human behavior at this time was influenced by the doctrines of psychologists John Watson and B. F. Skinner. Their behaviorist theories went something like this: "We may not know what goes on inside the brain, but we can certainly see what happens on the outside. Let's measure behaviors and learn to modify them with behavior reinforcers. If we like a behavior, reward it; if we don't, punish it."

We know today that the complex brain has its own reward system centered in the hypothalamus. This system lets us enjoy a behavior, such as achievement, and makes us want to do it again (Nakamura, quoted in Jensen, 1998). We know that self-efficacy is critical to motivation and to the energy to follow through with the work, even when things are not going well. Self-efficacy is based on past experiences with the learning that were positive. Success really does breed success, so provide opportunities for students to experience success and give feedback often.

The 1970s

The energy crisis, inflation, and the loss of the Vietnam War were components that affected the mood of the 1970s. Some of the fallout came in the following forms.

Divorce. Divorce became more acceptable in the 1970s, and with divorce came a breakdown in the family unit and the way of life associated with it. The American Association of School Administrators conducted a poll among Superintendent of the Year state finalists to find the 10 biggest changes in students today (Stratton, 1995). The number one concern for students today was listed as dysfunctional families.

Kids from dysfunctional families may suffer physical and/or emotional abuse. Some of the symptoms include withdrawal and depression, indifference, resignation, cynicism, aggression, truancy, poor grades, drug and alcohol abuse, and other negative behaviors.

More and more, it has become the role of educators to build in students a resiliency so that they can overcome their circumstances. Dr. Bruce Perry (1995), of the Baylor College of Medicine, says:

> Many children are raised in violent, abusive surroundings of which they have no control. The antidote is giving children a sense of self-worth and teaching them they are not helpless. If there's somebody out there who makes you feel like you're special and important, then you can internalize that with your view of the world.

It is important to note that the need to build resiliency in students is not confined to students from poverty, but encompasses students from all socioeconomic groups. There was a time when I would advise anyone working with students from generational poverty (i.e., poverty over several generations) that the most important way to reach those students is to build a relationship first. I still believe this, and it is a pivotal point to those who would help us work with students from poverty, such as Feuerstein (1980), who say, "For students from generational poverty to learn, a significant relationship must be present." However, having also worked with students from affluent backgrounds, I have come to realize that, with today's dysfunctional families, students from affluence also come to us with broken hearts, broken promises, and broken families, and that it is important that they also have a significant relationship to achieve at a high level.

Perhaps the legacy of the 1970s and the prophecy of the time that was to come can be summed up in a popular book of the time. In *The People Puzzle* (1979), Morris Massey wrote, "The proliferating flock of teachers, doctors, psychologists, counselors, social workers, and juvenile court officers . . . assumed the family's main function: raising children." He was speaking of the 1970s, but he could have been speaking of the decades to come.

The Equal Rights Amendment. The Equal Rights Amendment, the Thomas-Hill hearings, and a change in the face of America were to bring us to a time of so-called political correctness and an awareness of the need for training in gender and multicultural understanding.

Watergate. Watergate and the ensuing scandals brought down a president and created a loss of confidence in government and in those in high office. Scandals shadowed those in high office in the years to come and spilled over into Wall Street and the fiber of industry. These events would trigger a society in which, in this decade, there is a larger gap between the haves and the have-nots.

The 1980s

The beginning of the 1980s was a time of great prosperity, especially for the young. Then, political scandal once again changed the atmosphere.

Economic Woes. The savings-and-loan crisis burst the economic bubble of many. The recession that followed led to a heightened sense of mistrust and cynicism. To make ends meet, both parents entered the workplace. Some even took two jobs to help buy the American dream. With that change, children often went home after school to no parental supervision. The term *latch-key children* became a label for these students. Stratton (1995) says:

> Many argue that today's students are growing more disconnected from their families, their communities, and even from themselves. They seem to feel they are entitled to success, rather than having to earn it. And when they don't become successful, they claim they are victims of a society that has turned its back on them. This attitude transcends racial, ethnic and gender lines, and is further evidence of our cultural crisis, our moral laxity, some believe.

The 1990s

Media Changes. The 1990s were characterized by an electronic media explosion. Technology changed all of our lives and became a part of the day-to-day activities of our students. Because of budget restraints and an often inadequate understanding of "what to buy," schools remained well behind the real world in providing adequate technology opportunities in schools. We were teaching multimedia kids with 1950s technology in many cases. Caine and Caine (1997) put it well:

> Take a close look at American teenagers. For a moment, let time run backwards to deprive teenagers of gadgets that are in some way dependent on electricity. One by one, we remove the television, the CD player, the computer, the videodisc, the radio, tape player, record player, electronic games, airplanes, air conditioning and automatic heating, shopping in large malls, and the opportunity to acquire large numbers of possessions. How well do you think our teenagers could cope? How would their lives be different? And what about our own? One of the only places that would reflect scarcely any difference in the scenario we've painted—and that would be operating largely as it did more than 50 years ago—would be the local school.

A Thriving Market. The 1990s was also a time of bull market ventures, in which many profited. The buying of houses, cars, second homes, and luxury items were possible for those in the right jobs. Technology made overnight millionaires of many young entrepreneurs. As resources, jobs, and those who had the means moved to the suburbs, the inner cities were left to those who were trapped by economics or other influences.

The Demands on Education to Keep Up. Educational resources became thin as more and more demands were made on schools by legislators and business. National standards and testing were demanded as proof that schools were meeting the needs of students. The demands of teaching, lack of resources, lack of support systems, lack of appreciation by the public, and many other factors led to the migration of teachers out of education and into other fields.

Teacher Shortage. The teacher shortage begun in the 1990s worsened in the 2000s and has led to a national crisis in education and a rethinking of the way that we prepare and mentor new teachers. Predictions for teacher shortages at the turn of the century were ominous.

Other factors from the 1990s that have influenced education and society in general include the following:

- The Clarence Thomas–Anita Hill hearings changed the workplace and schools forever in regard to sexual harassment.
- The bombing of the Alfred P. Murrah Federal Building in Oklahoma City was the first of many shockwaves related to the vulnerability of Americans.
- The growing number of AIDS victims has made us all aware of the human vulnerability to diseases previously unknown.
- The school shootings in Boulder, Colorado and other schools throughout the country have led to a renewed need for programs to make schools safer and to identify troubled students.

WHY LOOK AT THE PAST?

We look at the past so that we can understand the influences on education today; but, beside this obvious answer, we look to the past so that we can recognize old ideas and attitudes.

I have included the information in the previous sections because there may be times when you hear or observe other teachers using methods or reasoning that matches former times but does not match today's students. These teachers may even try to convince you that their way is the best way, but I want you to know why those methods usually fail. For example, you may hear that it is not teachers who must change their methods to match today's students, but the students themselves who must change to meet our methods. A teacher may say, "It is my way or the highway." That theory may have worked in the 1950s and early 1960s, when the work force welcomed unskilled labor, but it does not work in this highly skilled society where all students must have an education and specific skills for jobs. Besides the fact that the law says we will teach all students, by relegating students to failure because they do not learn "our way" cheats those students and society of productive, self-reliant individuals.

Almost every secondary school has teachers who believe that the only method for teaching is through lecture, with the teacher as the imparter of knowledge. Yet we know from brain research that at least 87% of the students in the classroom today are not auditory learners (Jensen, 1998). So, any teacher who relies on lecture as the only method of teaching has decided to teach to only 13% of the students in the classroom. These teachers often have high failure rates, which they blame on their students' poor motivation to learn.

You may even come across someone who believes that intelligence is fixed at birth and that we can only do so much with students. The truth is that we come into this world ready to learn at a high level and that environment works in tandem with the brain to develop a human being that is highly capable. Environment is important to the developing brain, but it is not nature or nurture; it is nature *and* nurture (Jensen, 1997).

Students today are not the same as students ten years ago, much less fifty years ago. Today's students live in a multimedia world that is not limited by boundaries of the United States. They are more aware, more outspoken, and more demanding than past generations, and it takes a teacher with motivation and high energy to meet the challenge they produce.

The 2000s has already proven to be a time of great change in this country. We have become vulnerable for the first time to enemies outside our borders; we have become embroiled in war and the economy has proven fickle. For the first time in quite a while, the middle class has suffered major changes in their financial situations with the reversal in the stock market of the telecommunications industry and the loss of jobs by professionals. The chasm between the haves and the have-nots seems to have grown enormously. While the inner city in many places is on the decline, those with the ability to do so are building houses larger than ever before.

As we look at the students who come to us from poverty, it is fitting to look at what constitutes poverty today. It is not just a matter of money. Payne (2001) says that poverty is "the extent to which an individual does without resources." She further defines resources as financial, emotional, mental, spiritual, physical, support systems, and relationships. For example, financial resources involve the ability to buy the goods and services needed to survive and more. A support system means having people who serve as a backup when we are not able to purchase goods and services for ourselves. *Relationship* refers to appropriate adult behaviors that model for students what constitutes appropriate behavior.

To what extent can we, as educators, help students to obtain resources in these seven areas? I am convinced that the more we can do that, the greater the possibility that we can solve inner-city educational problems.

2

How Are
We Diverse?

Diversity is differences. There are many differences among students within one classroom, much more within a school. In this global society, it is not unusual to find a school in which there are as many as 30 different languages spoken and in which there is a vast difference among students in terms of socioeconomic standing. In Chapter 1, I listed an important difference among our students in terms of the ability to obtain the goods and services (resources) necessary for success. For the purposes of this chapter, we will look at the following differences:

- Differences in learning styles or modalities
- Differences among socioeconomic groups in regard to how they view the resources that affect schools
- Differences in race/ethnicity

WHY IS IT IMPORTANT TO EXAMINE DIFFERENCES?

The single most important influence on the climate in the classroom is the teacher. The teacher can create a classroom where there is chaos and a general disrespect for others or a classroom where there is a sense of community and an appreciation for the gifts that everyone brings to the educational process. The responsibility is not all the teacher's, but a large part of what happens begins with the beliefs and commitment that the teacher brings to the classroom.

As we select materials for our classrooms, we must take into account the differences that usually appear in our schools. What is the racial makeup of the class? Our materials and books should reflect that makeup by using pictures, illustrations, and quotations that bridge the races. Materials and other resources should appeal to both genders and, as teachers, we should be sure that students are called on equally. I was once observing in a middle school science classroom in which the teacher only called on the male students to answer questions. The underlying message was that science was for boys. I also visited a classroom where the minority students' desks were in the hallway. The attitude was blatantly biased.

The most important step in working with a diverse classroom is for the teacher to first examine his or her own attitudes about differences. McCune, Stephens, and Lowe (1999) recommend that teachers make a "concerted effort to avoid stereotypical expectations":

> To meet this challenge, teachers can begin by developing good teacher-student relationships. Teachers need to develop an awareness of practices common in various cultures, so that when children behave in a manner consistent with their culture, the behavior will not be misinterpreted. Nevertheless, teachers should discuss with students that some behaviors are acceptable at home but not at school.

Certainly, history has taught us that if we are to narrow the achievement gap in urban schools, we must have teachers who "have a clear sense of their own ethnic and cultural identities and who communicate high expectations to all students, along with the belief that all students can succeed" (Zeichner, 1996).

DIVERSITY OF MODALITIES

Sousa (1995) defines modalities as three types of learning styles. While students can learn in any of the three styles, most have a learning preference or style that comes easier for them. This is especially important when working with students who are experiencing difficulty learning. If we teach and re-teach using the same learning style that is not compatible with a student's mode of learning, the chances are that we will not reach that student.

Different learning styles and modality preferences tend to run in various ethnic and cultural groups. For example, students from the inner city tend to be more hands-on, kinesthetic learners. This reflects the culture from which they come, which relies on learning by doing. In contrast, there are cultures (particularly some Eastern cultures) in which students learn by listening. A teacher who will be successful with students in urban schools where there is a mixture of cultures will use various tactics for teaching that include a variety of resources. Such a teacher does not rely on only one modality or tactic for teaching, but provides information in a variety of contexts. As Zeichner (1996) says, successful teachers "focus instruction, guiding students to create meaning about content in an interactive, collaborative learning environment" and "provide a scaffolding that links the academically challenging and inclusive curriculum to cultural resources that students bring to school."

Society tends to identify intelligence by looking only at those who can take in information quickly, process it efficiently, and retrieve it from long-term memory when needed. Sprenger (2002) notes that students who take in information slowly but retrieve it quickly are usually labeled as overachievers. Students who take in information quickly but retrieve it slowly are often labeled as underachievers.

In order for us to store and use information, that information must have meaning, and meaning, is closely related to the way in which we take in information. If we would narrow and close the achievement barriers forever, we must pay attention to the ways in which we can help various cultures and ethnicities that have not been successful in the past make better use of the systems that control the intake, processing, and retrieval of information. Let's begin with the way that we take in information: Being able to take information in quickly and efficiently is tied to several factors, among them the learning modalities. The three modalities most often used in the classroom are auditory, visual, and kinesthetic.

Auditory Learners

The modality least used by students is auditory. Auditory learners are those who remember best information that they hear (Tileston, 2000). These students make up 20% or less of the classroom. They like lecture, adapt well to it, and tend to be successful in our traditional schools. Some other character-istics of auditory learners, according to McCune et al. (1999), are that they

- Like to talk and enjoy activities in which they can talk to their peers or give their opinion
- Encourage people to laugh
- Are good storytellers
- May show signs of hyperactivity or poor fine motor skills
- Usually like listening activities
- Can memorize easily

It is important to note that even auditory learners cannot listen to lecture all day, every day without problems. They need opportunities to talk about the information and to share their ideas so that the information becomes personally mean-ingful to them. The work of Sousa (1995) shows that adult learners tend to fade out mentally after about 15 minutes of lecture only to fade back in after 10 minutes of "down time." If you have ever been in a meeting that was being presented by lecture you may have noticed this happening, even though the topic might have been one of interest to you.

For students, we normally calculate the amount of time that they can listen at one time by their age. In other words, students who are nine years old will listen for about nine minutes before they fade out. Teachers who enjoy lecture can still lecture if they learn to break up the lecture into manageable chunks of time. Talk to your class for ten minutes, and then have them do something with the information before going back to another chunk of lecture. The activity may be as simple as having the students talk to each other about what you have just said, or it might be a guided practice activity. The point is to keep their brains actively involved in the learning. *Breaking Ranks* (National Association of Secondary School Principals [NASSP], 1996) provides this advice: "When possible, students should take an active role in their learning rather than as passive recipients of information passed on by textbooks and by teachers who do little more than lecture."

Ideas for meeting the needs of auditory learners include the following:

- Direct instruction, in which the teacher guides the learning through the application of declarative (what students need to know) and procedural (what students can do with the learning) objectives
- Peer tutoring, in which students help each other practice the learning
- Activities that incorporate music
- Group discussions, brainstorming, and Socratic seminars
- Specific oral directions
- Verbalizing while learning, including the use of self-talk by the teacher and the learner
- Cooperative learning activities that provide for student interaction. Because cooperative learning also includes movement, more students benefit from its use.

Visual Learners

The largest group of learners in the classroom are visual learners (Jensen, 1997). Visual learners need to see the information and to understand how things work. We could probably raise math scores all over the country today if we could find more ways to help these students *see* how math works. For visual students, drawing the problem or using nonlinguistic organizers (such as mind maps) helps them to see the problem or issue. For these learners, the axiom "I'll believe it when I see it" is absolutely true.

Use visuals often in your teaching and help students to develop mental models by using a variety of nonlinguistic organizers. Examples of nonlinguistic organizers include concept maps, fish bones, mind maps, and prediction trees. *What Every Teacher Should Know About Effective Teaching Strategies* (Tileston, 2004a) provides numerous examples of nonlinguistic organizers: For that reason, I am only including one example here. Figure 2.1 is an example of a concept map for science class. Because the brain naturally seeks patterns, these organizers employ a brain-compatible method of teaching that works for all students.

McCune et al. (1999) provide a list of some of the characteristics of visual learners. Visual learners are those who

- Have difficulty understanding oral directions
- Experience difficulty remembering names
- Enjoy looking at books or drawing pictures
- Watch the speaker's face
- Like to work puzzles
- Notice small details
- Like for the teacher to use visuals when teaching
- Like nonlinguistic organizers, because they help these students to see the information

Ideas for meeting the needs of these students include the following:

Figure 2.1 Visual Model: Mind Map

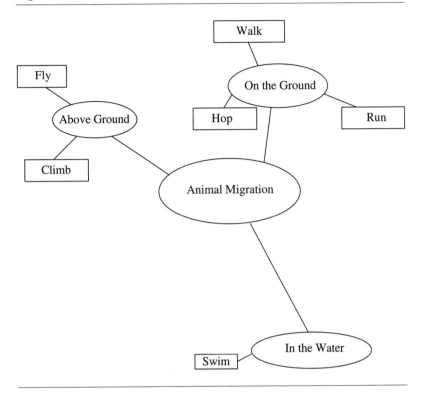

- Using visuals when possible
- Using models, puzzles, and DVD tapes
- Demonstrating the learning, when appropriate
- Including activities in a mind-game format
- Showing patterns in the learning

Kinesthetic Learners

Kinesthetic learners are those who need movement and touching. The students in the classroom who are often off task, who tend to talk to their neighbors, and who go to the pencil sharpener or trashcan at every opportunity are usually from this group of learners. These are the students who will say, "If you want me to learn how to do it, give it to me and let me work on it." They learn by doing and work well in a setting in which students work in small groups or in a classroom that incorporates such methods as discovery learning. Payne (2001) says that many urban learners fall into this category.

It is easy to see why many traditional teachers are having difficulty with these students. They need manipulatives, tactile materials, and the opportunity to try things out. A wise teacher will provide opportunities for movement in the classroom and will make use of tactile materials and manipulatives whenever practical. Instead of just talking about slope in math class, combine government and math by giving students the federal guidelines for handicapped ramps and have them measure or see if the ramps around school meet the specifications. Instead of talking about World War II, take the students on a scavenger hunt to the library to find information on people, places, and battles from that era. A variety of teaching tools will go a long way toward preventing learning problems in the classroom.

Some other characteristics of kinesthetic learners, from McCune et al. (1999), are that such students

- Need the opportunity to be mobile
- Want to feel, smell, and taste everything
- May want to touch their neighbor as well
- Usually have good motor skills, may be athletic
- Like to take things apart to see how they work
- May appear immature for their age group
- May be hyperactive learners.

Ideas for working with these kinesthetic learners include

- Using a hands-on approach to learning
- Providing opportunities to move
- Using simulations, when appropriate
- Bringing in music, art, and manipulatives to expand the learning
- Breaking up lecture so that verbal communication by the teacher is in manageable chunks

- Providing opportunities for learning through discovery when appropriate
- Using such techniques as discussion groups or cooperative learning so that these students have an opportunity to move about and to talk with their peers

It is important to note that the greatest number of discipline problems comes from this group, and a wise teacher will incorporate tools to keep this group actively involved.

Implications

It is unrealistic to think that we could meet the needs of all students for every activity, every day. The key is to provide a variety of activities. Once students are in our classrooms for a while, they learn the tricks that allow them to do minimal work. They divide up the assignments, divide up the homework, or find shortcuts in our routines. So, change up your routine; the brain likes novelty, and, by providing the learning in a variety of formats, we are more likely to teach to all students.

DIVERSITY OF SOCIOECONOMIC STATUS

Wang and Kovach (1996) argue that, while *Brown v. Board of Education of Topeka, Kansas* "made equal access to public education the law of the land," the accomplishments of the last few decades have "fallen far short of the vision of a universal school system that provides all children with equal access to success in school." They go on to say, "Census data from the 1990's show that the United States leads the industrialized world in numbers of children living in poverty." This is reflected in such legislation as the Goals 2000: Educate America Act, the School-to-Work Opportunities Act, and the reauthorization of the Elementary and Secondary Education Act.

Yancey and Saporito (1994) found that children from inner-city neighborhoods are more likely to contract everything from measles to tuberculosis to lead poisoning. As poverty rises, both children and young adults are more likely to be crime victims, to receive inadequate health care, and to suffer from a variety of physical, psychological, and social traumas. These circumstances place children at risk of educational failure and, by necessity, place schools at the center of interconnected social problems.

While the achievement gap, as identified on standardized testing and other measures, is a national problem, it is a problem that can be solved—but the solutions need to begin early, prior to the child entering the first grade. Researchers, such as Williams (1996) and Wang and Kovach (1996), remind us in the literature that the problem is not a one-stop fix, but involves community support and early intervention.

Certainly, the trend in the United States for all adult members of a family to work and to leave children to care-givers at daycare facilities for long hours has had its toll on our nation's children. Add to that the fact that the workday has become longer, that competition for jobs is stiffer, and that we have a nation of children who do not get much one-on-one time with an adult. Kotulak (1996) has found that, when caregivers talk to infants during the first three years of life, the children's IQ levels are higher: In his study of 43 Kansas City families, he found that children who were talked to the most had "strikingly higher IQs than children whose parents didn't talk to them very much." Kotulak also found that "children in white-collar families hear 2,100 words per hour on an average day, compared to 1,200 words per hour in the average work-ing-class family, and 600 words per hour in the average welfare family." By age four, the difference has become pro-nounced, with "children in welfare families having 13 million fewer words of cumulative language experience than the average child in a working-class family."

Jensen (1998), quoting the work of Healey, says that the evidence points to the fact that children today are not as prepared for school today as they were two generations ago. He cites more children in households with fewer resources, less early motor stimulation, more exposure to drugs and medications, and fewer natural foods as the culprits. All of these factors become enlarged as we look at children from poverty. Since school readiness begins in the womb, as infants are exposed to poor nutrition, drugs, and smoking from conception, schools are seeing more and more students with learning difficulties. Jensen (1995) says that the embryo, at its peak, generates brain cells at the rate of 250,000 per minute. No wonder so many children are experiencing difficulty from birth. Jensen further states, "The evidence suggests that emotional intelligence develops early and the school years may be a time of last resort for nurturing emotional literacy." Moreover, he says that the relationship between an infant and its primary caretaker is important in determining whether the child develops learning problems: Since we learn much of our emotional intelligence in the first year, it is important that children be given guidance in cause-and-effect situations.

According to Payne (2001), students from poverty have predictable characteristics of which the teacher should be aware. These students live in the moment rather than planning for the long term. They will work hard for a teacher they like and may get mad or quit if they don't like the teacher. Families from poverty believe that education is important but see it as an abstract entity, whereas middle-class families value education as a means to jobs and financial stability. Families from wealthy backgrounds see education as a tradition for maintaining connections.

What Can Schools Do?

"It used to be that we thought the brain was hard-wired and that it didn't change . . . [but] positive environments can actually produce physical changes in the developing brain," says Frederick Goodwin, former director of the National Institute of Mental Health (quoted in Kotulak, 1996). Dr. Goodwin emphasizes the importance of the environment on the brain, calling the environment the food for the brain's development: "You can't make a 70 IQ person into a 120 IQ person, but you can change their IQ measure in different ways, perhaps as much as 20 points up or down, based on environment" (quoted in Kotulak, 1996).

Marzano (1998), working with the research at Mid-continent Regional Educational Laboratory (McREL), says that certain teaching strategies, such as helping students to link new information to information they already know or providing specific feedback often to students as they work, can make a dramatic difference in student success: Just saying "good job" is not enough. Feedback should be diagnostic and prescriptive, should be given often, and should be sincere. As a matter of fact, telling students that they did a good job when they know that they did not do their best work may have a negative effect on the students' learning.

As teachers, we can ensure that our classrooms have the kind of environment that is conducive to feeding the brain. Jensen (1997) advises that, as educators,

> We can most influence the "nurture" aspect of students. Because of that, we must follow a cardinal rule when it comes to appreciating how the brain reacts to certain influences: Start by removing threats from the learning environment. No matter how excited you are about adding positives to the environment, first work to eliminate the negatives. Those include embarrassment, finger-pointing, unrealistic deadlines, forcing kids to stay after school, humiliation, sarcasm, a lack of resources, or simply being bullied. There is no evidence that threats are an effective way to meet long-term academic goals.

In addition, be proactive in your schools' efforts to provide free breakfast and lunch to those who need it. Older students are reluctant to use the program for fear of embarrassment: Help your school find ways to make the program anonymous for students who go through the lunch line. Be familiar with community resources that provide health care and dental and eye exams to those who cannot afford them and/or cannot afford insurance. Be proactive in helping to bring resources to your students and their parents by working with social, government, and community resources and with the leaders within the community.

DIVERSITY OF RACE/ETHNICITY

There are so many differences in terms of race and ethnicity that space does not permit describing the variety within our schools. The United States has become a nation of people from all parts of the world. It is not unusual to find 30 or more languages spoken in a new kindergarten group, and it is not unusual to find classrooms that reflect the vast differences found in the communities of this country. As Gibbs (1994) says,

> When the United States was originally founded to provide haven and opportunity to people from many countries, the metaphor of a cultural melting pot came into being. Now we realize that expecting all people to be assimilated into our dominant Western European culture has contributed to conflict, prejudice, and unequal opportunity for multi-ethnic populations.

Rather than trying to produce a melting pot, we must try to understand the cultures from which our students come and respect the differences. As teachers, we must first examine our own values and prejudices and how those affect our students. We must then help our students to respect one another and to accept the differences. When teaching about multicultural differences, it is also important that we look beyond the obvious diversity of food, climate, and dress to the things that truly make a difference.

As teachers, we want to make a difference in our students' lives. Many years of research have told us that one of the most important things that we can do to reach our students is to create a relationship. As a matter of fact, in some cultures, we will not be able to do much *until* we create that relationship. Being cognizant of the communities from which our students come—and the backgrounds of those communities—is important in how we approach those relationships. To do this takes time, but my friends who work with students from various backgrounds will tell you that you gain more time in the classroom once these relationships are established. The time you invest in creating a connection is worth it, because the kids are worth it.

3

Recognizing the Signs of Bias

G ibbs (1994) lists six types of bias to avoid in the classroom if we are going to truly respect and celebrate diversity among students. They are linguistic bias, stereotyping, exclusion, unreality, selectivity, and isolation. Using his terminology for the types of bias, let's look at what the implications are for the classroom.

LINGUISTIC BIAS

Linguistic bias includes any language that is dehumanizing or denies the existence of a certain group, such as females or males. It occurs when we teach history without acknowledging the contributions of minorities. Linguistic bias also occurs when a student's name is laughed at or deliberately mispronounced. Students who have difficulty with the English language or who have not mastered proper grammar may also experience linguistic bias when others snigger or belittle them. As a matter of fact, students new to this country often will not participate in class or answer teacher questions for fear of being ridiculed for their lack of English skills. Students may use what Payne (2001) calls *casual register*—the language they use outside of school or the way they talk—in the class-room or for writing papers instead of using proper grammar, formal register.

These students need to know that formal register is impor-tant to use in the classroom, because it will help prepare them to be successful in the outside world where use of formal register is the norm. You might have them write first in casual register and then translate it into formal register. Payne (2001) explains that, for students from poverty, language is in casual register because, for them, language is about survival. She goes on to explain that, for the middle class (around which schools are based), language is in formal register because it is about negotiation; for the wealthy, language is also in the formal register because, for them, language is about networking.

As teachers, we can minimize linguistic bias by setting the example and by not allowing put-downs in the classroom. We will want to discuss with our classes why it is important to treat others with respect. Our students are part of a very global world, and their roles as adults will not be limited by ocean boundaries. Directly teaching students about cultural differ-ences and how to work with other people is a real-world skill.

STEREOTYPING

The second type of bias that we should avoid is stereotyping. This is most often done in regard to male and female gender roles and to ethnic minorities. Encourage both male and female students to explore a wide range of activities and voca-tions, not just those traditionally open to men or women. For example, women today can be nurses and teachers, but they can also be attorneys and physicians if they choose. We also need to allow all students to demonstrate a variety of emotions.

When we select materials and books, we need to be cog-nizant of those that show minorities in the same kind of roles that would be shown for other students. For example, minorities perform leadership roles, job-related roles, and family roles, just as other segments of the population do. Help students to know that they have many choices in life and they are not limited by ethnicity, race, religion, or gender.

Anytime we give people choices, we empower them—and that sense of power is important. McCune, Stephens, and Lowe (1999) define *locus of control* as "the degree to which students feel that events they experience are under their own control (internal control), rather than under the control of other people or forces outside of themselves (external control)." As teachers, we strive to help students feel that they do have control over their success in school, and we make a conscious effort to help them see the relationship between what they do and their success. As McCune et al. (1999) say,

> Researchers believe that students will be more likely to engage in learning activities when they attribute success or failure to things they can control like their own effort, or lack of it, rather than to forces over which they have little or no control, such as their ability, luck, or outside forces.

Payne (2001) has identified one trait often found in students from poverty: they feel a sense of hopelessness and lack of control over their circumstances. We are not born with this trait; it is acquired through our environment. When students believe they have no control over their lives or their circumstances, they are more likely to drop out mentally, to be unmotivated, and to become depressed or even a discipline problem. As teachers, we have the power to give them hope and to give them some control over the circumstances in our classrooms. Allow students to help shape the rules or norms for your classroom, ask their opinions and advice on issues, and give them opportunities to reflect on and evaluate their own learning. Jensen (1997) says, "Our brain generates different chemicals when we feel optimistic and in control. These endorphins insure pleasure, the 'flow state' and intrinsic motivation."

EXCLUSION

The third type of bias to avoid is exclusion. Exclusion is simply the lack of representation by a group. It can also be the removal of a group from the larger group based on race, ethnicity, religion, or gender. A science teacher calling only on male students to answer questions or pulling the desks of minority students into the hallway are good examples of this type of bias. We must be careful as we call on students to answer questions that we call on a variety of students—and that we look students in the eye when we speak to them.

One of the most unfortunate ways that schools have excluded students of minority races and students with learning differences is to isolate them into special programs. I understand that students with special needs often require the services of professionals trained to help with their needs or handicaps; those are not the students to whom I refer here. I refer, instead, to students who are relegated to compensatory programs because they are poor or belong to a minority group, and so an assumption is made that they must need additional help. When we make those kinds of assumptions, we often get what we expect: Students are not expected to do well, so they don't do well.

Wang and Kovach (1996) say, "The mean reading score of a school's students can be predicted by their aggregated rates of childhood poverty and the various epidemiological problems. The more a school draws from poor neighborhoods riddled with social problems, the worse its students perform academically." Heller, Holtzman, and Messick (1982) say, "Students from ethnic and language minority backgrounds often are resegregated by a variety of pullout remedial or compensatory education programs." Often, what these students actually need is individual help, not a special program.

Many of us learned in our college classes about the controversy over nature versus nurture. Are we born with a fixed intelligence? Which is more important, our genes or our environment? Current brain research indicates that it is not nature *versus* nurture but rather nature *and* nurture. We are all born into this world hot-wired to learn and to learn at a very high level. If you don't believe me watch a two-year-old for a while: Children at that age are constantly exploring, tasting, smelling, watching, listening to, and verbalizing with the world that they are trying to grasp.

Why, then, do some students come to school without the necessary prerequisites for success? That is where nurture comes in to play. Learning should be encouraged from a very young age—but because of consequences and stresses placed on many home environments, parents are too exhausted, too stressed, or too ill to provide the nurturance that is needed. Add to that the fact that many children today go to daycare from the time they are old enough to leave the house. While many daycare facilities are excellent and provide wonderful reinforcement for children, many are understaffed and under-trained to provide the kind of nurturing needed for maximum development.

Students once thought to have learning problems may simply need encouragement to succeed and the individual nurturing to help them catch up with their peers.

UNREALITY

The fourth type of bias is unreality or the misinformation about a group, event, or contribution. One of the most famous studies in education points up this type of bias. Teachers were given new students, all of average intelligence. However, some teachers were told that their students were above average in intelligence, some were told their students were below average. At the end of the experiment, it was found that students who were expected to do very well did very well and students who were expected to do poorly did poorly.

In the teachers' lounge, in the hallway, and in faculty meetings, other teachers may share with you their opinions of students in your classroom. Smile and thank them, but lean on hard data and the demonstration of understanding that you see in your classroom. Let your students know that you believe in them and that you expect their best.

One school year, the teachers in my school started the year by telling students that this school year was a whole new ballgame. It did not matter what they had done in our classrooms last year, did not matter what their brother or sister had done. Beginning that year, we expected them to do their best work and we were not going to accept anything less than excellent work. As a matter of fact, we gave work back to them if it was not done well and provided additional help for them outside of the regular class time to redo their work. As a result, the quality of student work went up, and scores on state and national exams went up as well.

Ask yourself, "What are my expectations for my students?" Make sure that you have high expectations for all students, not just the pretty ones, not just those from the same ethnic group as you, and certainly not just those the group in the teachers' lounge told you would make it.

SELECTIVITY

The fifth bias is selectivity or the single interpretation of an issue, situation, or conditions. Help your students to see things from more than one perspective and to find more than one way to solve a problem. According to Payne (2001), students from poverty often laugh when disciplined. This comes from survival on the streets, where to show fear could literally cost them their lives. The role of the teacher is not to show intolerance for this reaction but to help the student to know that, although that reaction may be appropriate on the street, in the larger world, to laugh at your boss when reprimanded would probably cost you your job. Students may need to be taught the proper way to respond in the world beyond the streets. This is one of the ways that we build resiliency in our students.

In addition, we must be open to differing opinions and differing perspectives. Helping students to look at situations from varying points of view will help them to be better problem solvers. Often, understanding the underlying problem is half the journey to finding the solution. We find the underlying problem when we understand different perspectives.

ISOLATION

The sixth bias is isolation or the separating of groups. In the classroom, it is important to build a camaraderie among the students that fosters communication and acceptance. In a small school experiment, in which we actively built teams of students within each classroom (from elementary school through high school), we were surprised to find that students did not really know each other unless they happened to be on an athletic team together or to be friends outside of class. If that was true of a little school, how much more true it must be in large schools.

It takes a conscious effort to build rapport in a classroom, and it can only be done if students have an opportunity to talk with each other and to work together on the learning. Use the cooperative learning model, which requires grouping of students to mimic the make-up of the classroom. In other words, groups should include both male and female student and students from different ethnic groups. Johnson, Johnson, and Holubec (1987) say that students will never sit differently in the lunchroom if they don't sit differently in the classroom.

4

The Road to Closing the Achievement Gap

For years, we have been trying to close the gap in achievement between students from primarily Anglo groups and those from minority groups, specifically African American, Hispanic, and the urban learners. Based on the amount of time and resources put into this proposition, the results are poor. As stated in Chapter 2, the gap has widened in some segments. Zeichner (1996), along with Williams (1996), suggest that there are some factors that must be examined and dealt with if we are to close the gap forever.

THE URBAN ACHIEVEMENT GAP: FACT VERSUS FICTION

According to Williams (1996), the prevailing attitude in many circles is that there is an achievement gap because "urban schools and students can do no better." It is that attitude that has helped to create a laissez-faire attitude about not just narrowing the gap but also closing it. Until we look at the causes and the solutions to closing this gap forever, we will continue to have the spiraling effects of a limited education for the urban poor and in particular minorities, such as African Americans and Hispanics.

The solutions are not confined to the schools, but must be a part of a unified effort on the part of national, state, and local entities that work hand in hand with parents and the school. In order for poor students to be able to compete on a level playing field, they must have the quality health, nutrition, and other resources that are a part of the package of essentials provided to children who do not come from poverty. Wang and Kovach (1996) agree: "Narrowly conceived plans and commitment that focus only on schools will not solve the growing problems that must be addressed to ensure success of the many children and youth who have not fared well under the current system of service delivery."

Payne (2001) says that wealth is measured in the amount of available resources—not just money. Resources include such things as a strong support system, role models, the ability to work within the middle-class framework (which is the basis for most schools), being physically and mentally healthy, and having the money to purchase both goods and services. For those in poverty, the same resources are not as readily available as for those in more affluent surroundings. Until there is dialogue and cooperation among the political and social entities that can help to provide those resources, what can be done in schools is limited. It is limited, but it is very significant.

WHAT CAN TEACHERS DO?

While we have limited control over the decisions of political entities (we can vote for those who understand the problem and are willing to do something about it), we have direct control over what happens to the urban poor in regard to education in our classrooms.

Examine Our Beliefs

First, as a teacher, we must assess our own belief system about students. What preconceived ideas do we bring to the classroom? What are our expectations for our students? Do we bring biases to the classroom, and, if so, are we willing to rethink our biases based on what we have learned? Do we truly believe that all kids can learn and learn at a high level?

Do Not Tolerate Bias

Second, we must be determined that we will not tolerate belittling or demonstrations of bias in our classrooms and that we will be consistent about enforcing that idea.

Help Students Know Each Other

Third, we need to incorporate ideas for helping our students get to know each other and to be able to dialogue with each other in nonaggressive formats. Use icebreakers, such as the Find Someone Who tool in Form 4.1, at the beginning of school. In the Find Someone Who tool, students locate a different person for each of the questions listed. The first person to complete their list might get an extrinsic reward or special recognition. Sometimes, teachers vary this with a bingo-type format where students "win" when they get their paper signed either across or diagonally.

Build Resiliency

Fourth, help build resiliency in your students. In their book *Resiliency in Schools: Making It Happen for Students and Educators*, Henderson and Milstein (1996) provide a list of the characteristics of families, schools, communities, and peer groups that foster resiliency. Using their list as a guide, let's look at what we can do to help our students build resiliency.

Form 4.1   Find Someone Who . . .

Directions
- Give students a list of questions.
- Have student find other students in the room who can answer one of the questions. Students initial or write their first name by their answers.
- Require Students to get a different signature on each question.

FIND SOMEONE WHO . . .

Directions: Ask a different person to sign for each of the following. Find someone who . . .

Likes the same sport as you.

Has a blue car.

Has two brothers.

Plans to go to college in another state.

Had an unusual summer job.

Plans to become a lawyer.

Likes to work with computers.

Has a birthday in December.

Has been to Disney World.

Has an unusual hobby.

Variations
Directions: Use this tool as a review after material has been studied. Instead of personal questions, use questions about the lesson. For example

Find Someone Who . . .

Can define *denominator*.

One of the advantages to using Find Someone Who is that once a student finds an answer from another student, he or she becomes an expert on the topic and can sign someone else's paper.

Promote Close Bonds. Get to know your students as individuals rather than as a sea of faces that you encounter each day. Talk to them, give them individual attention, provide opportunities for discussion, and let them know that we are learners together. One of the most important things that a good teacher does is to promote self-confidence in students and to guide them to becoming self-directed learners. Think of your classroom as a community of learners with yourself included.

Provide opportunities for your students to get to know one another and to know you as their mentor, coach, instructor, and guide. Insist that students respect one another and you. First, be a model for this by showing respect for them, and then be certain that bullying, name calling, ethnic jokes or remarks, put downs, and disrespect are not tolerated in your classroom. Discuss with your class why you are doing this and be consistent. Don't let someone get away with negative or harmful behavior one day and enforce the rule on another day. Consistency is essential if real change is to come about. Steven Covey (1989) calls it the "28 day rule": If we practice a behavior for 28 days, it becomes internalized.

Value and Encourage Education. You will find that the value of education varies among your students and that much of what has influenced them has come before they entered your class. Payne (2001) says that all three socioeconomic groups—poor, middle class, and upper class—value education but in different ways. The poor value it but as an abstract entity. After all, when you are constantly trying to feed your family and keep the bill collectors away, education is not your primary concern. When working with students and parents from poverty, it is important to point out that education keeps them from being cheated and gives them an opportunity to solve economic problems. This is usually more productive than telling them that it is important to do well in school so they can go to the college of their choice. Kids from poverty tend to live in the here and now. What will education do for them right now?

Students from the middle class value education because it is a means to a better paying job and a good school. Students from the upper class view education as another rung in the networking ladder; for them, it is important to go to the right schools and to meet the right people who can help influence their future.

Understanding these differences in attitudes will give you a starting place for working with students and their parents to help them understand the importance of learning. For example, when people know how to use math effectively, they are less likely to be cheated, they are able to plan for the future so they can be independent, they have more opportunities to advance, and they are more likely to have the life they desire. Telling students that they need to learn so that they can go to the next grade or pass a test really does not do much for building long-term intrinsic motivation.

In addition, the brain learns more effectively those things that have meaning to the individual. According to Jensen (1997), the gatekeeper to the brain is "meaning": If the material has no meaning to the student, it is not likely to be remembered. The bottom line is to tell students up front why the lesson is important.

Other Guidelines. Other things we can do to build resiliency include:

- Using a high-warmth/low-criticism style of interaction
- Setting and enforcing clear boundaries (rules, norms, and laws)
- Encouraging supportive relationships with many caring others
- Promoting the sharing of responsibilities, service to others, "required helpfulness"

- Providing access to resources for the basic needs of housing, employment, health care, and recreation
- Expressing high, realistic expectations for success
- Encouraging goal setting and mastery
- Encouraging pro-social development of values and life skills, such as cooperation
- Providing leadership, decision-making, and other opportunities for meaningful participation
- Appreciating the unique talents of each individual

Promote Diversity

The fifth thing teachers can do is provide accurate information about cultural groups through straightforward discussions of race, ethnicity, and other cultural differences. This information should come from a wide variety of resources, not just the text or one resource. Kathleen Cotton's *Effective Schooling Practices* (1995) offers a summary of many resources. Be sure your information includes both cross-cultural similarities and cross-cultural differences: There are probably just as many differences within a culture as there are between cultures.

McCune, Stephens, and Lowe (1999) recommend that teachers keep the following ideas in mind as they promote diversity:

- Remember that cultural diversity in our schools and society can be recognized and appreciated without denunciation of Western values and cultural traditions.
- Recognize that there are as many differences within a group as there are between groups.
- Remember there is a positive correlation between teacher expectations and academic performance.
- Remember to hold high expectations for students, regardless of ethnicity, gender, or exceptionality.
- Remember that self-esteem and academic achievement go hand in hand.

- Remember that there is no single approach to meeting the educational needs of all children in a multicultural classroom.
- Remember that multiculturalism is not a "minority thing": It includes us all.
- Remember that human understanding is a life-long endeavor.

5

Which Teaching and Learning Strategies Make the Most Difference in Closing the Gap?

Unengaged teachers have been described as bored teachers who just go through the textbook and aren't thinking, teachers nicknamed Mrs. Ditto, or Mr. Filmstrip, teachers who taught one year, for 30 years, and teachers who barely know their students' names.

—K. S. Louis and B. Smith, "Teacher Engagement and Real Reform in Urban Schools"

Most of the teachers that I encounter as I work with schools through training do not fall into the description provided by Louis and Smith, although the dedicated teachers with whom I work tell me that those teachers are out there. I usually don't meet them because they are not the ones eager to go through training on new research. Fortunately, their numbers are dwindling. However, the number of teachers disillusioned with teaching seems to be on the increase with some schools reporting more than a 50% turnover rate annually. According to Louis and Smith (1996),

> Compared with teachers of more affluent children, teachers who work with students from poorer families are more likely ... to believe that their students bring behavior into the classroom that make teaching difficult. They also tend to believe that they have little influence over their students learning.

This chapter is devoted to providing information to help teachers of urban poor students guide their students to a greater success rate and at the same time provide efficacy for the teacher.

HIGH EXPECTATIONS: WHY THEY MATTER

As stated in Chapter 4, it is important to have high expectations for all students, not just those who exhibit good study skills. There are some obvious reasons as to why this is important. We know, for example, that when we have high expectations for students we are more likely to provide a rich and rigorous curriculum. There are deeper reasons that get at the heart of brain research on how our brains learn and remember.

THE ROLE OF THE SELF-SYSTEM IN LEARNING

The self-system of the brain is the gatekeeper to motivation and thus to learning. It is the self-system that directs our attention either toward the learning or toward daydreaming. In order to gain students' attention for the learning, we need to understand how this powerful system works and what we can do as teachers to activate the system in positive ways. There are several factors that affect the self-system of the brain. These factors automatically (without much conscious thought) direct our attention:

- *Self-attributes*—This factor refers to the way in which the student sees himself or herself. It is not limited to a one-dimensional view, but may vary with attributes. For example, a student may see himself one way in regard to athletics, another in regard to personal appearance, and yet another in regard to learning.
- *Self and others*—This factor refers to the way a student sees herself in regard to groups or units of people. In other words, what is her status in regard to her peers? To her family? To others?
- *Nature of the world*—This factor refers to the way in which the student sees himself or herself in regard to the world. Is the world friendly or hostile? Marzano (1998) says, "Within this category, an individual will have 'theories' about why specific events occur. These will include their beliefs about physical, emotional, sociological, and supernatural forces and how they came to affect specific situations and events."
- *Efficacy*—This factor deals with "the extent to which an individual believes she or he has the resources or power to change a situation" (Marzano, 1998). This belief is not just based on "I think and I feel," as in the case of self-attributes, but is based on facts derived from previous experiences. For example, if a student has had positive experiences with math in the past, she is more likely to have positive self-efficacy about math now. This is just one of the reasons why it is so important that students experience success in our classroom.
- *Purpose*—This category of the self-system has to do with the students' perception about their purpose in life.

Through the factors listed above, the student trying to decide whether to pay attention to the learning or to continue daydreaming will consciously and unconsciously activate the self-system by examining the importance of the assignment, utilizing the degree to which they have positive self-efficacy, and by taking into consideration his or her emotional response to the learning. Let's examine each of these in light of today's learners and what we can do as teachers to help students use this system to help them learn.

Importance

Marzano (2001) explains that "what an individual considers to be important is probably a function of the extent to which it meets one of two conditions: it is perceived as instrumental in satisfying a basic need, or it is perceived as instrumental in the attainment of a personal goal." Using these two measures, here are some ways that the classroom teacher can enhance the students' beliefs about the importance of the learning.

- Tell students up front why the learning is important. Explain how they might use it in the real world.

- Prior to the learning, build a connection between what the students are about to learn and what they already know.

The brain seeks connections, and where there are none, chaos can follow. *What Every Teacher Should Know About Effective Teaching Strategies* (Tileston, 2004a) provides numerous examples of how to make connections effectively. One of the teaching practices that seems highly effective in helping students make connections between previous and new learning is to begin by asking students to create a nonlinguistic organizer about the prior learning. This can be done in small groups or individually. A nonlinguistic organizer is a graphic picture of the learning that relies on structure rather than words. A mind map is an example of a nonlinguistic organizer. Chapter 4 provided an example of a mind map for science class.

What if I am introducing a unit of study for which my students have no prior knowledge? In that case, I must create the connection. Whistler and Williams (1990) use the example of introducing from the book *Henry Huggins,* by Beverly Cleary, at the elementary level: In this book, the main character finds a dog and brings it home only to have the owner show up and want his dog back. To build empathy (which is one of the skills necessary for understanding), a teacher might begin the lesson by asking students to tell what they would do in a similar situation. Whistler and Williams call this strategy "We'd Rather," and it places students into similar situations as the main characters to see what the student would do. They give children choices, such as to hide the dog, to give the dog back willingly, to pretend that you don't have the dog, or to work out an arrangement with the owner so that you can see the dog.

We can also make the learning personally important to our students by asking them to write personal goals for the learning. As teachers, we model this activity by making a visual model of our declarative and procedural goals (what we want to the students to know and what we want the students to be able to do as a result of the learning) for the unit or lesson. We should take the time to go over those goals with the students and then have them make two or three personal goals based on this information. By doing this, we not only provide a personal connection to the learning, but we provide a way for students to examine how well they are doing in their own work. Come back to these goals often and show students how to modify their personal goals when things are not working. Forms 5.1 and 5.2 are elementary and secondary examples of how this might look.

Efficacy

The exercises in Forms 5.1 and Form 5.2 also help to build efficacy in our students. By providing a way for students to self-evaluate their own learning, we provide a basis for them to monitor and adjust their work to succeed. We also build

Form 5.1   Elementary Example of Goal Setting

For the book *Bubba, The Cowboy Prince,* I have provided some learning goals for you.

The declarative goals are that you will know:

- The sequence of events
- The importance of the sequence of events to the story
- The main characters and how they contribute to the story
- The main idea of the story

The procedural goals are that you will be able to:

- Compare and contrast Bubba with other versions of Cinderella
- Identify how the author uses humor
- Compare ways that the author uses setting, main characters, theme, and activities in unique ways as compared to the more traditional Cinderella
- Write your own version of Cinderella

What are some personal goals that you have made for yourself?

- I want to be able to identify how setting, characters, and theme are used in a variety of Cinderella stories so that I can make a decision about my writing.
- I want to create a humorous version of Cinderella that uses a funny animal instead of a person.
- I want to learn to use humor like the author of *Bubba* does.

---

self-efficacy by ensuring that students have positive experiences with the learning. One of the best ways of doing that is to provide consistent and constructive feedback often. Do not rely on blanket statements, such as "good going," to make a difference in self-efficacy. The work of Marzano (1998) shows

Form 5.2   Secondary Example of Goal Setting

For your lesson on John Hersey and his account of Hiroshima, I have set the following objectives.

The declarative objectives are that you will know:

- The definitions of the vocabulary associated with this lesson
- The responsibilities associated with impartial reporting
- The key attributes used by Hersey to report his accounts as an observer

The procedural objectives are that you will be able to:

- Infer information through generalizing, predicting, summarizing, and hypothesizing
- Analyze given information
- Create your own written product through synthesizing, organizing, planning, and problem solving

What are some personal goals that you have for the learning?

- I want to understand how to write impartially, even when everything around you is going wrong.
- I want to know when it is appropriate to write in an impartial way and when it is not.
- I want to be able to tell the difference between facts and opinions.
- I want the opportunity to write something from an observer's point of view. I don't know if I can do that.

---

that when feedback is consistent and when it is specific, the effect on student learning is huge. Without this process, the results may be disastrous. We may even be helping students to move backward in regard to success when we rely only on blanket statements or when we give praise that is not deserved.

Learned helplessness is a condition that develops over time when the person experiences failure after failure. This is a condition with which we deal when students come to us from poverty, from the negative effects of the urban city, and with only negative experiences with learning. It is important to note that learned helplessness is just that—it is learned by one's environment. Altering the perception and experiences of the learning can change it.

Emotional Response

Enough cannot be said about the importance of emotion on learning. Emotion has the power to shut down or to enhance quality learning. While it is important how each student feels about the learning, about the instructor, about the classroom, and about himself or herself in the learning situation, these feelings are critical to the urban learner. Inner-city poor will pay little attention in a classroom where they feel a threat—emotional, physical, social, or mental. The relationship with the teacher is paramount in reaching these students. This does not mean that the teacher must be their buddy, but rather that the teacher must exhibit understanding and warmth toward all of the students. Such a teacher seeks to understand the special problems of the urban learner, seeks to make connections for learners with various resources to enhance the students' lives, and to teach in a variety of ways so that all students are reached.

WE HAVE THEIR ATTENTION—NOW WHAT?

Once students begin a task or decide to pay attention, the metacognitive system of the brain takes over. This system relies heavily on goals that have been set by the student (either consciously or unconsciously) and on whether the student will follow through when things are not going according to plan.

Since the metacognitive system is going to set goals with or without our input, it is to our advantage as teachers to promote quality goals by explicitly demonstrating how we set objectives for the learning and by asking our students to make personal goals. We can enhance the work of the metacognitive system in our students by doing the following:

1. Set goals for the learning and share those goals (in writing or in pictures for young learners) with students.

2. Explicitly show students how to set personal goals for the learning.

3. Provide linguistic and nonlinguistic organizers as a guide to help students set goals.

4. Demonstrate to students how we use positive self-talk as we work through problems. This is especially important when personal goals are not going well and we must work through or revamp our plans to carry out the goals. One of the major complaints about all students—and about urban learners in particular—is that they exhibit impulsivity both in behavior and in learning. We control impulsivity by having a plan and by knowing what to do when the plan is not working. This ability must be taught to our students; they will not come to our classrooms with that knowledge. We can only know that the plans are not working if we walk around the room often to see and hear what students are doing and by providing very specific feedback.

5. Provide students with a rubric or matrix prior to the learning so that they know the expectations and so that they know what we mean by quality work. I am convinced that more students would work at a quality level if they know what that was. In *What Every Teacher Should Know About Student Assessment* (Tileston, 2004b), I talk about how to create rubrics and matrices for student work. We should never take a grade for a product, from homework to projects, without first giving

students a matrix or rubric that specifically gives them the expectations. To do otherwise is a "gotcha" and it is not fair. By providing a rubric or matrix up front, we take the personality out of the grading. The rubric states explicitly the expectation and the point value. If the student does the work, the student gets the grade; my personal feelings toward the student, his past work, or his behavior do not matter. This is one of the best ways that I know to begin to level the playing field for all students.

GENERAL IDEAS FOR COGNITION

I have discussed the importance of giving instructional strategies that affect the self- and metacognitive systems of the brain. The following detailed suggestions provide strategies specifically aimed at cognition.

Provide scaffolding to bridge the gap between how students learn in the home/neighborhood environment and how they learn in school. Zeichner (1996) says there are two ways that we can build this scaffolding. One is by incorporating the students' culture and language into the classroom. The other is by explicitly teaching students about the culture of the classroom (which is built, in part, on the middle-class structures). Let's look at what this means in terms of classroom instruction and the environment.

Incorporating the Language and Culture

Before we can incorporate the languages and cultures of our students into our classroom, we must make ourselves aware of what they are. We need to have an understanding of the neighborhoods from which our students come, as well. Next, we must use the resources that our students bring with them to enhance the learning. For example, storytelling is a part of many cultures and, in particular, of Hispanic and African American households. Teachers who can put learning into the context of a story are helping these students to learn in a modality that is comfortable and familiar to them.

Another way that we can enhance the learning of our students is to use examples from their world. Provide writing opportunities that incorporate the experiences and the culture from which they come. Provide examples that incorporate those things with which they are familiar. I talk about Kay Toliver in many of my books. Kay Toliver taught math in an inner-city school with some tremendous results. When she taught fractions to her students, she didn't say, "You need to know this so that you can be successful." Instead, she told them specifically how learning fractions would help them to be successful. For example, knowing fractional parts will keep them from being cheated when they buy food by the slice, such as pizza. There is a big difference between 1/16 of a pizza for $1.00 and 1/4 of a pizza for the same amount of money. Students from the urban areas tend to live in the present: They want to know how the learning will help them now.

Students from the inner city often use a form of language referred to by Payne (2001) as *casual register*. Basically, casual register is the language of the street. It is unrealistic to believe that students will come to us knowing the more formal register of the classroom. Payne even suggests that, for these students, we might allow them to first write in the casual register and lead them to rewrite in the more formal register of the classroom and professional writing.

Teachers who know their students and their culture will understand that students who do not speak English well (i.e., English language learners) may be embarrassed to speak or read aloud in English in the classroom. They often can speak more words than we think because they exhibit shyness in the classroom when asked to speak. Use patience with these students as they become comfortable with their surroundings.

Also, know that English language learners often lack the language acquisition skills to process and embed English

Figure 5.1   Using Pictures and Symbols to Learn Vocabulary

Vocabulary word	Definition	Words, symbols, pictures to help me remember
Creating	Generating new products	 *A*
Analysis	Breaking whole into parts	
Problem solving	Clarify problem, generate solutions, test hypothesis, evaluate	C larify G enerate T est E valuate
Inference	Generalizing, predicting, summarizing	If . . . . .then

words into the long-term memory systems of the brain. We can help them to put information into long-term memory by relying on context and on visuals to help with the learning. Again, nonlinguistic organizers are a good way to help these students process information in the classroom. When learning vocabulary, I have used a visual organizer, using pictures with the words, to help my students learn the terms. Figure 5.1 is an example of a visual organizer for learning vocabulary when the primary language is not English.

Since the semantic memory system of the brain is the system that stores facts, vocabulary, places, and names, we can help English language learners by giving the words a symbol or connector to help the students store the information in a more appropriate context.

Explicitly Teaching the Culture of the Classroom

We cannot assume that students who come to us from poverty and from other cultures will automatically know and understand what Payne (2001) calls the "hidden rules" of the classroom culture. For the most part, these hidden rules are based on middle-class ideals and values. For example, we often tell students that they need to learn given material because it will help them get into the college of their choice or because it will make them more successful later on in life. While that is important for all students to know and believe, we must work with our students in terms of what is important to them. For many urban learners, survival is paramount, and they want to know how learning is going to help them now. How will it enhance their status with their friends? How will it help them to survive? How will it keep them from being cheated? Begin here, and then tell them that it will also provide opportunities for them in the future because you believe in them and that they are capable of great things.

Help students to understand that there is a set of behaviors and communication standards that work on the street and there is another set of behaviors and speech patterns that will make them successful in school and at work. Payne (2001) uses the example of a student who laughs when disciplined. The rule of the street is that you do not show fear—it could get you killed. However, when disciplined at school or when a boss talks to you about an error, to laugh is to show disrespect. We cannot assume that our students will know that information without explicitly being told the difference in what is acceptable on the street and what is acceptable in the classroom. This information is important for our students to know, and it should be delivered in a voice that is polite, friendly, and nonjudgmental—not in an authoritative or superior voice.

When students from the inner city misbehave, they need to know the other choices that they had and how to plan so that they are not impulsive in their behavior. The language of the street is physical and loud. These students may not have the resources to know how to react otherwise. In those cases, we must explicitly teach them the difference. Cooperative learning programs are a great way to teach some of these skills. Inner-city students tend to be visual and kinesthetic learners; they like movement and they like working with their friends. They need structure, however, or they will be a discipline nightmare. Just putting students into groups is not cooperative learning. Cooperative learning is very structured and incorporates social and emotional intelligence structures alongside the cognitive structures.

SOME ADDITIONAL THOUGHTS

Zeichner (1996) provides some additional advice for teachers working with urban poor that can help to narrow and close the achievement gap. The following are taken from his work and paraphrased by me.

As teachers, we must

- Truly believe and communicate to our students that all kids can learn—and that they are capable of quality learning, not just superficially covering the material.
- Provide a rich, high-level curriculum that gives all students equal opportunities in life.
- Help students to create meaning from the content through a variety of teaching techniques that take into consideration students' backgrounds.
- Provide meaningful learning tasks for all students.
- Provide the scaffolding necessary for all students to be successful.
- Help students to take pride in their heritage while also teaching them the hidden rules of society.
- Create a personal bond with each student and lead students to know that we believe they can learn at a high level.
- Provide a variety of resources in the classroom that take into account the heritage of our students.

How Do We Deal With Language Acquisition Skills?

English Language Learners, sometimes called Second Language Learners comprise a large and growing group of students in this country. As the face of urban learners changes, so does the role of the school in meeting the challenges of a diverse population that may not speak the English of the classroom. These learners usually fall into one or more of the following groups:

1. Students who have come to this country speaking one or more languages that does not include English. These students may speak little or no English and English is usually not spoken at home.

2. Students who have come to this country as refugees from other countries. For these students language may not be the only hurdle they must jump. These students, called LFS students (Limited Formal School) may not have had much if any formal education due to the conditions in the countries from which they come. According to Teachers of English to Speakers of Other Languages also called TESOL (2001), these students often exhibit the following characteristics:
   - "Pre- or semiliteracy in their native language
   - Minimal understanding of the function of literacy
   - Performance significantly below grade level
   - A lack of awareness of the organization and culture of school"

3. Students who speak the informal language of the streets and who do not speak the more formal register related to school and the workplace.

The first step for the teacher is to identify the stage of language acquisition in which these students fall. TESOL (2001) provides three stages of language learning and the expectations for each of the stages. These stages are fluid; a student may be one stage in a certain setting and another stage in a different setting. For the classroom teacher, identify the stage or stages that are representative of your classroom.

Beginning Stage

At this stage, students have little or no understanding of the English language. Most of their communication is nonverbal. As they begin to grasp some words these students may initiate questions or statements by using a single word or simple phrases.

These students construct meaning through nonprint such as graphs or other non-linguistic examples. Although they may construct meaning from some words, the construction of understanding is incomplete

Intermediate Stage

At the intermediate stage, students have a small vocabulary of essential words and phrases that cover their daily activities. They understand more than they are able to speak although they still require a great deal of repetition from the speaker. At this stage they are using language spontaneously but in a limited way. For example, they may know the basic words to express themselves but lack the terms to make their wishes or thoughts more finite. Their speech is simple and may contain grammatical errors. While they are able to construct more knowledge from texts than at the beginning level, there is still a need for nonlinguistic examples to assist in the understanding.

Advanced Stage

At the advanced stage, students are able to communicate in the daily activities. There will still be the occasional structural and lexical errors of the other stages. They can use English in new settings but complex or abstract structures are still difficult. At this level, the student should be able to read with fluency and to locate facts within text. They may, however, have difficulty with texts that do not present information in context. Occasional comprehension problems may persist.

General Guidelines for Teachers

The following guidelines are offered to assist the classroom teacher as he/she works with students who do not speak the English Language register.

- Students who are learning English move through various developmental stages. The rate at which a student moves is based on the student's background and comprehension of their first language, the degree to which they have been exposed to a formal educational setting, their learning styles, and motivation. According to ESOL (2001), it may take a language learner as long as five to seven years to acquire English language skills comparable to native English speakers.
- Students will learn language at a quality level when they are given the opportunity to use language in interaction and in meaningful activities. We help to give meaning to the new learning by building on the culture and learning style of the student. Without meaning, there is little motivation to learn. We need to provide personal meaning to all students and in particular English Language Learners. Most students learning a new language, learn more efficiently when they can learn in context. For example, a class is beginning a new unit in reading in which they will read a story about Johnny Appleseed. For this unit, the teacher begins with a discussion of apples. She asks students to share what they know about apples by providing opportunities for them to discuss how they know about apples from experiences they have had. She is giving apples a context – personal experience.
- Provide many opportunities in the classroom for interaction among the students. By doing this, the teacher is

helping students not only acquire the English language acquisition needed for cognitive development, but for social development as well.

- Give feedback often. Language learners need to have goals and they need to know if they are meeting those goals.
- As the students progress in their use of language add more challenging activities. Remember that the problem is not intelligence but language acquisition.
- As we look at reading, listening, writing and speaking, remember that students may be in different stages within these four components of language. For example, a student may be in the beginning stage of writing, an advanced stage of listening and an intermediate stage of reading at the same time. Learning a language encompasses all four components and students do not learn them in a linear fashion. For example, students do not learn to speak first, write second, etc. Students move back and forth through reading, listening, writing and speaking as they acquire language skills.

6

Working With Diversity

A Teacher's Checklist

Checklist 6.1 is a good visual model to help you as you reflect on this book. Make a checkmark by the things that you have accomplished in regard to diversity. Since learning about diversity takes time, you may want to check those things that are true today, and go back periodically to see your growth.

Look for opportunities for networks with other teachers in your building and in other schools to support and encourage yourself.

Stalin supposedly said that he did not need armies to take over countries. He said to give him the country's children for one generation and he would have the country. Who has greater influence over society than teachers? Our influence has the power to change a new generation—for the better.

Checklist 6.1

The following checklist is offered as a guide for schools as they begin to look for ways to not only narrow the achievement gap, but to close it.

What will you do?

In my country and in my state, I will

- ❑ Be cognizant of the attitudes and plans of lawmakers and political candidates in regard to inner-city problems.
- ❑ Be an informed voter.
- ❑ Work for an alignment of federal and state resources to help the urban poor and to level the educational playing field.
- ❑ Be proactive in assuring that federal and state measures for success (i.e., testing) is free of bias or restrictions that single out any particular group.
- ❑ Work for national standards that take into account all students and that provide the resources for success— not just to the more affluent areas but also for all students and all teachers.
- ❑ Volunteer to serve on boards and committees, especially those that are setting policies for testing and for resources.

In the community, I will

- ❑ Become proactive to provide better health, mental, mentoring, physical, and fiscal resources for my students.
- ❑ Work with parents and other caregivers for solutions.
- ❑ Actively involve parents and members of the community in advisory groups.
- ❑ Set meetings at times that working parents can attend.
- ❑ Provide interpreters for parents who do not speak English.

(Continued)

- ❑ Take into consideration that some parents have come from countries where those in authority have not been fair or friendly. They may be wary of school personnel, especially if they are not citizens.
- ❑ Provide opportunities for my students to become proactive in their own communities with projects that include such activities as art, music, writing, starting a newsletter, or providing help at clinics or other community facilities.
- ❑ Because poverty is a matter of lack of resources, help students to increase the resources within their own communities.

In the hallways and within the school, I will

- ❑ Make good nutrition a priority.
- ❑ Emphasize good hydration for learning.
- ❑ Examine curriculum and books for examples of bias and work toward a plan for eliminating bias throughout the school.
- ❑ Set norms that include the respect for all people.
- ❑ Set norms that say learning is important.
- ❑ Provide advisory groups that include students as well as community people.
- ❑ Provide opportunities for after-school activities.
- ❑ Provide opportunities for additional resources that are a part of the school budget, such as nurses, counselors, and librarians.
- ❑ Make sure that the resources in my school are rich in culture and reflect the races and ethnicities of my students. While Martin Luther King Day is important, it should not be the only time of the year that we celebrate diversity.

(Continued)

- ❏ Be aware of students who are absent too much, in danger of dropping out, or in danger of failure.
- ❏ Provide an adult advocate for every student in the school. (This can be done through teams of teachers and senior students.)
- ❏ Fight for better conditions for my school if they are not up to par with other schools in my region.
- ❏ Be proactive in asking for the resources that my students need to be successful.
- ❏ Provide ongoing professional development that includes ways to reach students in my school and that examines the best practices, especially in regard to brain research and learning.

In the classroom, I will

- ❏ Set classroom standards that define expectations that all students will be respected.
- ❏ Bond with all of the students.
- ❏ Model the behavior that I expect of my students.
- ❏ Provide information to my students about resources available to them.
- ❏ Make my students aware of the need for good nutrition and hydration in regard to learning.
- ❏ Communicate caring and concern for all students.
- ❏ Communicate high expectations while keeping the threat level low.
- ❏ Help students to understand how their own brains work and how that affects all that they do.
- ❏ Build positive self-efficacy in my students.
- ❏ Teach the "hidden rules" to students and when they are used.
- ❏ Build positive self-esteem in my students.

(Continued)

- ❑ Provide a variety of teaching resources in the classroom that take into account the backgrounds, ethnicity, and race of my students.
- ❑ Use a variety of modalities in the classroom, especially visual and kinesthetic.
- ❑ Contextualize the lessons.
- ❑ Create experiences that help students make connections between prior learning and experiences and the new learning.
- ❑ Create opportunities for students to set personal goals for the learning.
- ❑ Explicitly show students how to use self-talk and other techniques to revise their goals when they encounter problems.
- ❑ Help students to complete work at a quality level.
- ❑ Provide specific and prescriptive feedback on an ongoing basis to students.
- ❑ Teach in a variety of ways so that students learn in the way that they are accustomed.
- ❑ Help students to make the transition from the language of the street to the language of the classroom.
- ❑ Provide opportunities for students to work together in heterogeneous groups.
- ❑ Emphasize the gifts that all students bring to the table.
- ❑ Recognize and overcome linguistic bias.
- ❑ Recognize and overcome stereotyping bias.
- ❑ Recognize and overcome exclusion bias.
- ❑ Recognize and overcome fragmentation/isolation bias.
- ❑ Recognize and overcome selectivity bias.
- ❑ Recognize and overcome unreality bias.

Vocabulary Summary

At-Risk Students

Students are labeled *at risk* when, because of circumstances, they are deemed to be more likely to encounter learning problems, to fail, to dropout, to be absent more often than other students, or to have more health problems than the general student population. The criteria for labeling a student as at risk vary from school to school, but may include any of the following factors:

1. Low socioeconomic status

2. Previous failure in school

3. Previous absentee record or health problems

4. Previous record of recurring discipline or other behavior problems

5. Identification for compensatory programs, such as Title I or special education

6. Migrant student status

7. Limited English proficiency or English language learner status

Not all schools use all of these criteria, but some of these identifying factors are usually a part of the program within a school. Ideally, being labeled as at risk will provide students with additional assistance in the form of tutors, emotional support, parent-teacher conferences, and frequent analysis of the student's records for signs of problems. Unfortunately, such assistance is the exception rather than the rule in most schools. Very often, students are labeled as being at risk, but little else is done beyond the label.

Teachman, Paasch, Day, and Carver (1997) say,

Clearly, poverty experienced during adolescence negatively affects the educational attainment of children. The role played by education in determining the economic and occupational success for Americans suggests longer-term consequences. The consequences of dropping out of high school are particularly drastic: over the past two decades, individuals with less than a high school degree have suffered an absolute decline in real income and have dropped further behind individuals with more education.

Bias

Bias is belief that something or someone is inferior or superior based on a set of criteria.

Classroom Climate

Classroom climate refers to two major areas within the classroom:

- The physical make-up of the classroom, such as lighting, color of the room, smell of the room, seating arrangement, visuals, and temperature.
- The emotional mood of the classroom, such as how students feel about the learning, the teacher, the other members of the classroom, and the positive as well as negative emotions within the class.

Direct Instruction

Direct instruction is instructional delivery primarily from the teacher that encourages a high level of learner engagement and requires structured, accomplishable tasks.

Under direct instruction, the teacher might follow these steps:

- Introduce the topic and the vocabulary necessary to understand the topic.
- Model, demonstrate, or discuss the information.
- Provide opportunities for students to practice the learning in a very structured environment with the teacher providing feedback.
- Provide opportunities for students to work independently using the new information.

Diversity

Diversity refers to the ways in which we differ from each other, including gender, age, ethnicity, race, religion, exceptionality, and socioeconomic status.

English Language Learners

English language learners are students whose primary language is something other than English and who have a limited knowledge of the English language. Because students who do not know the words cannot activate the semantic memory system (which stores words), it is important that teachers activate other memory systems by using visuals and movement.

Ethnicity

Ethnicity refers to the ethnic identity of a group, such as Native American, Asian American, or Caucasian.

Ethnocentrism

Ethnocentrism is the belief that one's own ethnicity is superior to others.

Exceptionality

The term *exceptionality* refers to the characteristics that make us different, such as handicapping conditions or giftedness.

Heterogeneous Grouping

Heterogeneous grouping is a technique for putting students into groups that reflect the makeup of the class rather than by ability or interest. For example, if a classroom is 50% minority students and 50% Caucasian, the makeup of the groups would be 50% minority and 50% Caucasian. Johnson, Johnson, and Holubec (1994) say in *Cooperative Learning* that students will never sit in different groupings in the lunchroom unless they sit differently in the classroom.

Hidden Rules of Society

According to Payne (2001), every social class has *hidden rules* that are only known to that class. For example, for children from poverty, the most important possession is people: for the middle class, it is things, and for the wealthy it is one-of-a-kind objects, legacies, or pedigrees. Money for those in poverty is to be spent; for the middle class, it is to be managed; and for those from wealth, it is to be invested. Where one went to school distinguishes the social rich from the merely rich and those below. In terms of time, those in poverty live for the moment, the middle class look to the future, and the wealthy believe in traditions and history. It is interesting to note that each class believes that everyone knows their hidden rules, but the truth is that we tend to know the rules of our group only.

Imaginary Audience

Students preoccupied with their own physiological changes often assume that others are equally intrigued by these changes in appearance and behavior. They may even feel that others (the *imaginary audience*) are staring at them, waiting for them to make a mistake. They reason that if everyone is watching, then it is imperative to be, to look, and to act just right. That means wearing cool clothes and fitting in with the appearance of the group. The implication for the classroom is that teachers should be aware of the group dynamics going on and should not do anything to bring undue attention or embarrassment to the student. It is very important to the students that they fit in.

Intrinsic Motivation

Intrinsic motivation is internal motivation associated with activities that are rewarding in themselves. An example of intrinsic motivation would be a student who reads a book because he or she wants to learn more about the subject or character or because the student loves to read.

Some researchers believe that the frequent use of rewards in classrooms is a deterrent to intrinsic motivation.

Learned Helplessness

Learned helplessness is the learned belief, based on such circumstances as poverty, that one is doomed to failure. According to Michael Harrington (1962) in *The Other America*, "The new poverty is constructed so as to destroy aspiration; it is a system designed to be impervious to hope."

Learning Environment

The learning environment comprises the mood, tone, and physical conditions that surround the learning.

Locus of Control

Locus of control refers, according to McCune, Stephens, and Lowe (1999),

> to the degree to which students feel that events they experience are under their own control (inner control) rather than under the control of other people or forces outside of themselves (external control). Researchers believe that students will be more likely to engage in learning activities when they attribute success or failure to things they can control like their own effort, or lack of it, rather than to forces over which they have little or no control, such as their ability, luck or outside forces.

Teachers should help students, especially at-risk learners, link their successes to something they did to contribute to the success. When this occurs, the students develop self-efficacy and the confidence that they have the power within themselves to be successful.

Melting-Pot Theory

The *melting-pot theory* was the belief popular in the United States for many years that those who come to this country should assimilate and blend into the dominant culture. Most Americans have come to believe that we need to embrace cultural differences rather than try to make everyone like us.

Minority Group

A *minority group* is a racial or ethnic group that has the least number within a society.

Modality

Modality is the way in which students take in information. The three common modalities are:

- Visual. Visual students need to see the material, and, in math, they need to see how the math works. Simply telling them the material is not enough. The largest number of students in the classroom is in this group. Could we raise math scores across the country if we could find more ways to show students how math works?
- Auditory. Auditory students want to hear the new information. They usually like to listen and take notes. The smallest number of students in the classroom is in this group.
- Kinesthetic. Kinesthetic students need hand-on experiences. They also need movement or you will lose their interest and they may become discipline problems.

Motivation

Motivation is the willingness or drive to accomplish something. It may be extrinsic (driven by outside forces, such as the promise of a reward) or intrinsic (driven from within).

Multicultural Education

Multicultural education is a process designed to increase awareness and acceptance among people of different cultures.

Nondiscriminatory Testing

Nondiscriminatory testing is testing that takes into account a student's cultural and linguistic background.

Personal Fable

Personal fable refers to the belief that "my life is different from every one else's, so no one can understand how I feel or think." This view of life may result in either a feeling of isolation (usually predicated by a changing body) or a willingness to engage in risky behaviors (e.g., "others get pregnant, but it won't happen to me").

Self-Concept

Self-concept refers to the way in which an individual sees himself or herself.

Self-Efficacy

Self-efficacy is the self-confidence to be successful. According to Cummings (2000), "Self-efficacy, the belief that you have the power to accomplish a given task, determines whether a student attempts the task or avoids it." Cummings goes on to say that self-efficacy can be instilled in students when teachers do the following:

- Teach goal setting
- Encourage positive self-talk
- Break long-term projects into small steps
- Measure the success of each small step
- Involve students in the self-evaluation of their effort

Self-Esteem

Self-esteem is the value a person sets on his or her self-worth.

Self-Fulfilling Prophecy

A *self-fulfilling prophecy* occurs when one's biased beliefs about what should occur influences the results to confirm one's expectations.

Researchers Good and Brophy (1966) provide the following examples of how teachers often treat students based on their perception of them. Teachers may

1. Seat high achievers across from and down the middle of the room.

2. Seat low achievers far from the teacher.

3. Seat low achievers near each other in a group.

4. Give fewer nonverbal cues to low achievers during instruction (e.g., smile less often, maintain less eye contact, etc.).

5. Call on high achievers much more frequently than on low achievers.

6. Use a longer wait time for responses from high achievers.

7. Fail to stay with low achievers when they attempt a response.

8. Criticize low achievers more frequently for incorrect responses.

9. Praise low achievers more frequently for inadequate public responses.

10. Provide low achievers with less frequent and less specific feedback regarding their responses.

11. Demand less work and effort from low achievers.

12. Interrupt performance of low achievers more frequently.

13. Talk negatively about low achievers more frequently.

14. Punish off-task behavior of low achievers and more frequently ignore it in high achievers.

Socioeconomic Status

Socioeconomic status is the relationship of an individual's economic status to social factors, including education, occupation, and place of residence.

According to Teachman et al. (1997),

Income accounts for about 50% of the difference in educational attainment of children raised in one- and two-parent families. The remaining differences for one-parent children are attributed to receiving less parental supervision (especially from fathers) and having less "social capital" because they move more frequently.

Voices

According to Payne (2001), we all have three *voices* that we use throughout our lives: *the child voice, the parent voice,* and *the adult voice.*

The child voice has the following attributes: It is defensive, victimized, emotional, whining, strongly negative, nonverbal, and has a losing attitude. It may also be playful and spontaneous.

Example: "Quit picking on me."

The parent voice tends to be authoritative, directive, judgmental, evaluative, demanding, punitive, sometimes threatening, and has a win-lose attitude. It can also be loving and supportive.

Example: "You do as I say."

The adult voice tends to be nonjudgmental, free of negatives, factual, and often speaks in a question format. It has a win-win attitude.

Example: "In what ways could this be resolved?"

Using the parent voice with children from poverty often causes the situation to become more heated. Payne (2001) says to use the adult voice and to begin to teach children from poverty how to use that voice beginning in about the fourth grade. Payne calls the adult voice the "language of negotiation." It is the voice most used in business and in the school setting, and it should be taught to children from poverty to help them to be successful in those worlds.

Vocabulary
Post-Test

At the beginning of this book, you were given a vocabulary list and a pre-test on that vocabulary. Below are the post-test and the answer key for the vocabulary assessment.

VOCABULARY POST-TEST

Instructions: For each question given choose the best answer or answers. More than one answer may be correct.

1. The belief that one group of people is superior to other groups is called . . .
   A. The melting-pot theory
   B. Ethnocentrism
   C. Exceptionality
   D. Diversity

2. Diane Madden is a teacher at East Middle School, where she teaches eighth-grade American History. Ms. Madden talked with teachers from the seventh grade prior to the beginning of school and asked them to give her their opinion about which students will be A students and which students will not put forth effort in her classroom this year. Ms. Madden's actions are most probably connected to . . .
   A. Ethnocentrism
   B. The melting-pot theory

    C. Exceptionality

    D. Self-fulfilling prophecies

3. Students who come from generational poverty are usually . . .

    A. Auditory learners

    B. Visual learners

    C. Kinesthetic learners

    D. Declarative learners

4. Students who believe that they just have bad luck in school may be suffering from poor . . .

    A. Diversity

    B. Locus of control

    C. Self-efficacy

    D. Self-esteem

5. Students who believe that they can succeed because they have succeeded in the past are practicing . . .

    A. The auditory modality

    B. Locus of control

    C. Self-efficacy

    D. Extrinsic motivation

6. Teachers who tell students that they will get candy for good work are using . . .

    A. Locus of control

    B. Intrinsic motivation

    C. Self-fulfilling prophecy

    D. Extrinsic motivation

7. Marci, a student in South High School, has experimented with drugs with her friends. Although she has been told that the drugs are addicting and can lead to harmful behavior, Marci believes that she is immune to bad things happening to her. Marci is practicing . . .

    A. Imaginary audience

    B. Locus of control

    C. Personal fable

    D. Self-fulfilling prophecy

8. Students who have lived in situations of great stress over time often experience . . .
   A. Imaginary audience
   B. Self-fulfilling prophecy
   C. Exceptionality
   D. Learned helplessness

9. Teachers who teach in a variety of formats so that they teach to all races and ethnicities are practicing . . .
   A. Contextualization
   B. Ethnocentrism
   C. Pluralism
   D. Indirect teaching

10. English language learners (ELLs) . . .
    A. Are considered to have low socioeconomic status
    B. Speak a language other than English as their primary language
    C. Are often shy in class
    D. Have low intrinsic motivation to learn

11. Raul is in Mr. Vasquez's math class at Moors Middle School. Raul is struggling because he cannot grasp some of the math concepts being taught. Mr. Vasquez has added graphic organizers to help students like Raul learn more successfully. Raul is probably what kind of learner?
    A. Kinesthetic
    B. Visual
    C. Auditory
    D. Dual skill

12. Which of the following are used to determine at-risk students?
    A. Low socioeconomic status
    B. ELL status
    C. Previous failure
    D. Ethnicity

13. Marty came to school on Friday with red streaks in his hair (just like his two best friends). Marty is exhibiting . . .
    A. Personal fable
    B. Self-efficacy
    C. Imaginary audience
    D. Self-fulfilling prophecy

14. When students become what we expect them to become, it is called . . .
    A. An imaginary audience
    B. A self-fulfilling prophecy
    C. Self-efficacy
    D. Personal fable

15. Most students in the classroom are what type of learners?
    A. Auditory
    B. Visual
    C. Kinesthetic
    D. Intrinsic

16. *Diversity* means . . .
    A. Differences
    B. Ethnicity
    C. Exceptionality
    D. Bias

17. The belief that people moving to this country should become like us is called what?
    A. Exceptionality
    B. Ethnocentrism
    C. Multicultural
    D. The melting-pot theory

18. Intrinsic motivation is triggered by . . .
    A. Relevance
    B. Stickers
    C. Emotions
    D. Relationships

19. Kelvin Waters has difficulty completing tasks once he begins. Research on which topic would be most helpful for him?
    A. The metacognitive system
    B. The self-system
    C. The cognitive system
    D. The procedural system

20. Which of the following is part of classroom climate?
    A. The lighting in the room
    B. The amount of tension in the room
    C. The way the room smells
    D. The socioeconomic status of the students

VOCABUALRY POST-TEST ANSWER KEY

1. B		11. B	
2. D		12. A,B,C	
3. B, C		13. C	
4. B, C, D		14. B	
5. C		15. B	
6. D		16. A	
7. C		17. D	
8. D		18. A,C,D	
9. A, C		19. A	
10. B, C		20. A,B,C	

References

Bartelt, D. W. (1994). The macro ecology of educational outcomes. *School-Community Connections, 3*(1), 2–3.

Caine, R. N., & Caine, G. (1997). *Education on the edge of possibility.* Alexandria, VA: Association for Supervision and Curriculum Development.

Cotton, K. (1995). *Effective schooling practices. A research synthesis* [1995 update]. Retrieved May 31, 2003, from http://www.nwrel.org/scpd/esp/esp95toc.html.

Covey, S. R. (1989). *Seven habits of highly effective people.* New York: Simon & Schuster.

Cummings, C. (2000). *Winning strategies for classroom management.* Alexandria, VA: Association for Supervision and Curriculum Development.

Feuerstein, R. (1980). *Instrumental enrichment: An intervention program for cognitive modifiability.* Glenview, IL: Scott, Foresman.

Gibbs, J. (1994). *Tribes.* Santa Rosa, CA: Center Source.

Good, T. L., & Brophy, J. E. (1996). *Looking in classrooms* (3rd ed.). New York: Harper and Row.

Harrington, M. (1962). *The other America.* New York: Simon & Schuster.

Heller, K., Holtzman, W., & Messick, S. (1982). *Placing children in special education: A strategy for equity.* Washington, DC: National Academy of Science Press.

Henderson, N., & Milstein, M. (1996). *Resiliency in schools: Making it happen for students and educators.* Thousand Oaks, CA: Corwin Press.

Jensen, E. (1995). *The learning brain.* Del Mar, CA: The Brain Stone.

Jensen, E. (1997). *Completing the puzzle: the brain-compatible approach to learning.* Del Mar, CA: The Brain Stone.

Jensen, E. (1998). *Introduction to brain-compatible learning.* Del Mar, CA: The Brain Stone.

Johnson, R. T., Johnson, D. W., & Holubec, E. J. (1987). *Structuring cooperative learning lesson plans for teachers.* Edina, MN: Interaction Book.

Johnson, R. T., Johnson, D. W., & Holubec, E. J. (1994). *Cooperative Learning in the classroom*. Alexandria, VA: Association for Supervision and Curriculum Development.

Kotulak, R. (1996). *Inside the brain*. Kansas City, MO: Andrews McMeel.

Louis, K. S., & Smith, B. (1996). Teacher engagement and real reform in urban schools. In B. Williams (Ed.), *Closing the achievement gap* (pp. 120–147). Alexandria, VA: Association for Supervision and Curriculum Development.

Marzano, R. J. (1998). *A theory based meta-analysis of research on instruction*. Aurora, CO: Mid-continent Regional Educational Laboratory.

Marzano, R. J. (2001). *Designing a new taxonomy of educational objectives*. Thousand Oaks, CA: Corwin Press.

Massey, M. (1979). *The people puzzle*. Reston, VA: Reston Publishing.

McCune, S. L., Stephens, D. E., & Lowe, M. E. (1999). *Barron's how to prepare for the ExCET* (2nd ed.). Hauppauge, NY: Barron's.

National Association of Secondary School Principals. (1996). *Breaking ranks: Changing an American institution*. Reston, VA: Author.

Payne, R. K. (2001) *A framework for understanding poverty*. Highlands, TX: Aha! Process.

Perry, B. D. (1995). *Children, youth, and violence: Searching for solutions*. New York: Guilford.

Sousa, D. (1995). *How the brain learns*. Reston, VA: National Association of Secondary School Principals.

Sprenger, M. (2002). *Becoming a wiz at brain-based teaching: How to make every year your best year*. Thousand Oaks, CA: Corwin Press.

Stratton, J. (1995). *How students have changed: A call to action for our children's future*. Arlington, VA: American Association of School Administrators.

Teachman, J. D., Paasch, K., Day, R., & Carver, K. (1997). Poverty during adolescence and subsequent educational attainment. In G. J. Duncan & J. Brooks-Gunn (Eds.), *Consequences of growing up poor* (p. 443). New York: Russell Sage.

Tileston, D. W. (2000). *Ten best teaching practices: How brain research, learning styles, and standards define teaching competencies*. Thousand Oaks, CA: Corwin Press.

Tileston, D. W. (2004a). *What every teacher should know about effective teaching strategies*. Thousand Oaks, CA: Corwin Press.

Tileston, D. W. (2004b). *What every teacher should know about student assessment*. Thousand Oaks, CA: Corwin Press.

Wang, M. C., & Kovach, J. A. (1996). Bridging the achievement gap in urban schools: Reducing educational segregation and advancing resilience-promoting strategies. In B. Williams (Ed.), *Closing the achievement gap* (pp. 10–36). Alexandria, VA: Association for Supervision and Curriculum and Development.

Whistler, N., & Williams, J. (1990). *Literature and cooperative learning: Pathway to literacy.* Sacramento, CA: Literature Co-Op.

Williams, B. (1996). A social vision for urban education: Focused, comprehensive, and integrated change. In B. Williams (Ed.), *Closing the achievement gap* (pp. 148–160). Alexandria, VA: Association for Supervision and Curriculum Development.

Yancey, W., & Saporito, S. (1994). *Urban schools and neighborhoods: A handbook for building an ecological database* [Research report]. Philadelphia: Office of Educational Research and Improvement, National Center on Education in the Inner Cities, Temple University Center for Research in Human Development and Education.

Zeichner, K. M. (1996). Educating teachers to close the achievement gap: Issues of pedagogy, knowledge, and teacher preparation. In B. Williams (Ed.), *Closing the achievement gap* (pp. 56–76). Alexandria, VA: Association for Supervision and Curriculum Development.

Index

CORWIN PRESS

The Corwin Press logo—a raven striding across an open book—
represents the happy union of courage and learning. We are a
professional-level publisher of books and journals for K-12 educators,
and we are committed to creating and providing resources that
embody these qualities. Corwin's motto is "Success for All Learners."